Freezing Food on a Budget

Cooking for one, two or more

SARA LEWIS

ACE BOOKS

© 1996 Sara Lewis
Published by Age Concern England
1268 London Road
London SW16 4ER

Design and typesetting GreenGate Publishing Services, Tonbridge Kent

Cover photograh Steve Lee

Printed in Great Britain by Bell & Bain Ltd, Glasgow

A catalogue record for this book is available from the British Library

ISBN 0–86242–207–8

Other books by Sara Lewis Published by ACE Books:
Eating Well on a Budget
Entertaining on a Budget
Healthy Eating on a Budget

Contents

Recipes

Author's introduction

We all need to watch the cost of the weekly food bill, but if you've a growing family and an elderly relative to cook and care for, resources may be stretched to the maximum.

Over 80 per cent of households now own a freezer, but many of us do not use it to it's full potential and see it more as a frozen cupboard. Your freezer can help to save money. Don't pass up that greatly reduced joint, two for the price of one or other irresistible offers just because you haven't time to cook it. Freeze the food and cook when you do have time.

This book aims to maximise your time and funds so that you can produce tasty, filling suppers for all the family. Whether you are stocking your widowed fathers freezer or dropping dinner round to an elderly mother, you will never be stuck for what to serve with well over 100 budget-conscious recipes to choose from.

Batch cooking needn't be time consuming. Making up a batch of mince doesn't involve much extra work whether cooking for one, two or eight! Try to make up a few extra dishes at the weekend and freeze them away in handy one person portions. You can then defrost as many portions as you need giving you greater flexibility.

A freezer is invaluable if you can't get to the shops easily, perhaps you no longer drive, are not strong enough to carry heavy bags home or work full time. This book is also ideal for anyone about to have a baby when not only funds but time will be at a premium.

There are also lots of helpful background tips on running your freezer as efficiently and cost consciously as possible. Plus guidelines for storage times, defrosting times and most importantly what to do if your freezer accidentally defrosts.

Owning a deep freeze needn't mean a diet of fishfingers, chips and ice cream, but a wealth of tasty dishes for all occasions, from light lunches and suppers to hearty main meals and tempting teatime treats.

Sara Lewis

About the author

Sara Lewis is a cookery journalist and a qualified home economist, she is a freelance cookery editor on Practical Parenting magazine, has written two books on cooking for children and contributes regularly to Take a Break magazine. Sara has also written Eating well on a Budget, Entertaining on a Budget and Healthy Eating on a Budget, published by ACE Books. Married with two small children, her greatest love is to cook for family and friends.

Acknowledgement

A special thank you to my husband Andrew, who has tried and tasted all the recipes.
    I would also like to thank:

The Frozen Food Information Service
Bury House, 126-128 Cromwell Road
London SW7 4ET

Food Safety Advisory Centre
14 Soho Square, London W1V 5FB

The Department of Health

Lakeland Plastics Ltd
Alexandra Buildings
Windermere
Cumbria LA23 1BQ
Tel: 015394 88100

for supplying plastic freezer ware

Sara Lewis
June 1996

1 Why freezing makes sense

Cooking for a growing family and elderly relative day in day out can become a huge burden for the cook. Owning a freezer can seem like a lifesaver and can relieve the pressure of cooking three meals a day, on a daily basis. Why not cook two meals one day and have the second day off, or even a week's worth of meals for greater freedom.

Many older people feel comforted by routine and like their foods at specific times. This can seem frustrating for younger members of the family. By freezing food in one person portions the cook can simply reheat individual portions when required or leave instructions for timings and temperatures.

Cooking for one can also become rather tiresome, even depressing, particularly when recently widowed. It is better to cook when you feel in the mood and make enough for other meals to be enjoyed on days when you don't want to cook, perhaps after a day out with friends or when its raining and you can't get to the shops.

For the frail elderly, freezing one person portions can mean that one of the family can drop dinner round 'meals on wheels' style. This allows relatives to maintain regular contact and also ensures that the relative has a healthy diet while retaining much valued independence.

Freezing one person portions can also be extremely useful for a family where teenage children come and go at different times and prefer to heat up their own dinner, or perhaps where one member of the family works shifts and either needs to take a meal to work or to reheat something quickly when they return home.

Cutting costs

When working to a tight budget it is important to shop around. It is amazing how supermarkets and freezer centres vary in price, with many offering two for the price of one special offers in their bid to lure new customers. The problem with large supermarkets is that there is so much choice that it is very hard to pop in for a few items and to only come out with just those items. We must all have fallen into the trap of coming out with a trolley load when really a basket full was all we had gone in for!

If bulk buying, try to buy items that you know are good; it is no good buying four cans of special offer sardines if the family will only eat tuna. Check out large packs of foods too: they don't always offer the savings you would expect.

Shopping with a calculator can help you to keep a running total and also to compare value for money between brands and pack sizes. Although its helpful to go shopping with a list, this should remain flexible so that budget buys can be substituted to save money.

Shopping around your local street market for fresh produce can very often offer great savings and it is here that a freezer can come into its own. You may be able to pick up three or four heads of broccoli for a £1 or even three cauliflowers, but there is a limit to how much of each the family can eat per meal. Blanch and freeze them or make them into soups, pies or casseroles. Multiply recipes to make full use of bargain buys. Very often, market produce needs to be eaten immediately and once again a freezer can help here. Put what you can eat now into the fridge and freeze the remainder. Refer to p.15 for storage times.

Buying larger quantities of foods on offer will use up a large proportion of your weekly food budget. You may find it useful to keep a £5 or £10 note at the back of your purse for such moments and try to resist the temptation to spend it on anything other than food!

Cooking larger quantities also maximises use of fuel, particularly when slowly cooking a casserole. Why cook a meal for one when you can cook one for eight for the same cost in fuel.

Budget beaters

I   If your freezer's running low, then fill up empty spaces cheaply with bread, frozen veggies, cartons of milk, even clean newspapers.

2 Get the maximum use of space by freezing cooked casseroles and soups in plastic boxes lined with plastic bags. Once they are frozen into blocks, remove plastic box and stack bags.

3 There is no need to buy special containers: recycle yogurt pots, margarine tubs and ice cream cartons. For small quantities use sections of a plastic egg box.

4 Bulk buy reduced items in the supermarket at the end of the day. Look out for bargain priced cuts of meat and fish, but double check that they haven't been frozen already. Compare the prices of frozen meat and fish, which are often cheaper than fresh food and provide a welcome chance to treat yourself to something you didn't think you could afford.

5 Don't throw those dregs of wine or beer away, but freeze them in sections of an ice cube tray. Use them to flavour casseroles, pasta sauces and gravy.

6 Likewise with any beaten egg left from glazing pies. Transfer the cubes to a small plastic bag when frozen.

7 Freeze leftover egg whites in small containers, or sections of a plastic egg box. They are great for making meringues at a later date but do remember to label how many egg whites there are.

8 Don't throw away that chicken carcass: break it into pieces so that it is more compact, pack it into a plastic bag and freeze. Make it into chicken stock for soups at a later date.

9 Freeze any leftover Yorkshire puds wrapped in cling film. Reheat from frozen in a hot oven for 5 minutes.

10 Make decorative ice cubes with sprigs of herbs from the garden, leftover lemon or orange cut into quarter slices.

11 Freeze chopped herbs from the garden in yogurt pots. There is no need to defrost the herbs before use, just sprinkle them over dishes before serving.

12 Make stale bread ends into breadcrumbs with a liquidiser, food processor or grater and freeze in a plastic bag. They are great for sprinkling over fish pie, macaroni cheese and/or making into stuffings.

13 Whisk any leftover whipping or double cream with a little sugar. Pipe whirls on to non stick baking paper or foil lined baking sheet. Open freeze the whirls until solid. Pack them into a plastic box when frozen and use them to decorate desserts. Simply add a cream whirl to individual desserts and allow to defrost for 15–20 minutes.

14 Save the peel each time you eat an orange. Freeze the leftover orange peel in a plastic bag. Defrost and cut it into shreds, and add to a can of marmalade mix for cheap homemade marmalade or to spice up rock cakes or fruit cake.

15 Stamp any pastry trimmings into tiny shapes with cutters. Bake them and use them to float on soups. Or cut them into 3 inch (7.5 cm) rounds, press them into sections of a bun tray and make them into mini quiches. Freeze them in a plastic box.

16 Store fresh nuts in small plastic bags so that they don't go stale.

17 Freeze any leftover rice in plastic bags in individual portions. To reheat, remove bag, plunge rice into water and cook for 2–3 minutes.

18 Make your own bags of ready-grated cheese when cheese is on special offer. There is no need to defrost the cheese before cooking.

19 Freeze away seasonal fruit and vegetables when they are at rock bottom prices in pies, crumbles, vegetarian casseroles and soups.

20 Make the most of larger bargain buys: cook and freeze a big lasagne, casserole or other favourite for family gatherings or celebratory meals. This helps to spread time, effort and most importantly the cost, leaving the cook free to enjoy the special occasion too.

2 Buying a freezer

Over 80 per cent of households now have a freezer, or if not a freezer then an ice section in the fridge. For most, buying a freezer is not a new experience, but if family circumstances have changed or perhaps your deep freeze is now too big or too small for your requirements you may be thinking of replacing your existing model.

There are three main types available:

Upright freezers – these vary considerably in size, from under counter models, similar in size to a basic fridge to large 12–14 cubic feet models. Like a fridge they have front opening doors but with pull out baskets instead of shelves for easy loading and unloading.

Chest freezers – these too come in a wide range of sizes and tend to be cheaper than upright models. They have top opening lids with large roomy interiors, usually with a couple of small hanging baskets for everyday essentials. As there are no shelves as such it can be difficult to find foods, so pack similar foods in coloured plastic bags so they are easy to locate. Pack fragile foods in sturdy plastic boxes to prevent damage. Depending on the size chosen they will also take up more floor space. Try to avoid this design if you have a bad back as reaching to the bottom of the freezer may be difficult.

Fridge freezers – these are great if space is at a premium. They are available in a wide range of sizes with varying sized fridge and freezer sections. Most have automatic defrost. Some have two motors so you can turn the fridge off while on holiday and leave the freezer on, or turn off the freezer for cleaning and defrosting while the fridge is still in use, or vice versa.

Sizing up

Deciding on what sized freezer to buy can be difficult. So choosing a freezer to fit within your budget must be prime importance.

If you live alone or are a couple who plan to freeze only perhaps a week or two's supply of food then a 3–4.6 cubic foot freezer as part of a fridge freezer would be perfect. For a couple who wish to freeze homemade meals, frozen vegetables etc, then a 5 cubic foot under counter upright freezer or 6.4 chest freezer would be ideal. For a growing family a 7.6–11.1 upright freezer or similar sized chest freezer may be a better choice. Chest freezers are available in a wide range of sizes up to 18.1 cubic feet, but they obviously cost more to stock and run.

It is better to have a smaller jam packed freezer for the most efficient use of electricity. As a rough guide 1 cubic foot of freezer space will store approximately 20–24 lb of food depending on how it is stacked.

Check points

- Where will the freezer be sited? Measure the space in the kitchen; perhaps an upright freezer would be better here while a chest freezer would fit in the garage or under the stairs. Make sure you will have enough space to open the door. Avoid placing a freezer next to a cooker, hot pipes or in a hot lobby where the freezer will have to work hard to maintain low temperatures and so increase running costs.

- If you are planning to put the freezer in the garage make sure it is dry or the freezer will rust quickly. Rub the freezer with one or two coats of wax polish for added protection. Make sure the garage can be locked or choose a freezer that has a lock already fitted. The contents of a freezer can be extremely valuable, not just in terms of cost but also in time spent batch-cooking.

- Is the floor strong enough? This is not such a problem if you are buying a small under counter freezer but for larger models check before buying.

- Have you an electric point nearby? The socket should preferably be a single point so that there is less chance of the freezer being turned off accidentally. Label the plug or tape over the socket as a safety precaution.

- How much do you want to spend? Shop around for the lowest prices, check the discount warehouses, electrical shops or department store end of season sales. Look at your local paper for good second hand deals or visit your local auction room, but don't forget that the price you bid will have VAT and buyer's premium added.

What to look for when buying

- Check that there is a fast freeze facility.

- Are the controls easy to understand and could a child or grandchild interfere with them?

- Choose a freezer with an in-built thermometer and easy to read temperature indicator.

- Check that you can easily reach the top shelf of an upright freezer or the bottom section of a chest freezer.

- If you are buying a chest freezer check that it has a drainage hole, so that you do not have to bail it out when defrosting.

- Is it a frost-free model?

- Look for rollers which will help to move the freezer for easy cleaning and adjustable feet to level the freezer if the floor is uneven.

- Look out for a lock if you are storing the freezer in a garage.

- Check the number of baskets and other equipment, eg ice cube trays, defrost scraper.

- Is it a good price?

- Can the freezer be delivered?

Making the most of your freezer

Although it is an expensive piece of kitchen equipment initially, once stocked, a standard 5 cubic foot under counter freezer will use 1.1 units of electricity every 24 hours, costing between 5 and 7p depending on the area in which you live.

Stocking the freezer

Stocking a new freezer can seem a dauntingly expensive prospect. Draw up a list of the kinds of food that you eat regularly and aim to freeze:

- Some ready frozen raw ingredients, such as frozen chicken portions, a whole chicken, few packs of mince, chicken livers or lambs liver, fish fillets.
- Some fresh foods eg a few pounds of sausages, separated into smaller useable packs; sliced bacon.
- Some emergency foods such as a few blocks of cheddar cheese or bags of grated cheddar; tub of margarine; sliced loaf; a few ready prepared main meals and puddings.
- Some bags of frozen vegetables – no freezer would be complete without a bag of frozen peas, while frozen beans make a much cheaper alternative to fresh and likewise frozen sweetcorn is much cheaper than canned, with the added advantage that you need only take out of the freezer the amount that you need.

Add a tub of ice cream, a bag of homemade crumble, a few packs of frozen puff pastry and you're prepared for anything. If funds or freezer contents are running low, a few extra loaves of bread and a few cartons of milk also make handy fillers.

If you're new to freezing its easy to get carried away when shopping:

- Shop around – a freezer offers the chance to buy cut price bargains, but make sure to buy foods that you like and will use. Its no good buying four packs of liver on special offer if everyone detests it!

- If buying brand names choose products of good quality. Don't bulk buy brands of inferior quality – they may not be such a bargain in the long run.

- Don't buy something in bulk if you haven't tried it before.

- Check prices carefully: large packs do not always mean great savings and remember that they can take up valuable space in the freezer, so limiting the range of foods that can be stored, especially in a small freezer.

- Defrost the freezer and sort through food every 3–4 months so that you know exactly what's there.

Get packing

To ensure that your freezer is running as efficiently as possible make sure that it is as full as possible. Pack foods close together and try to group similar foods together.

Freeze foods in a plastic bag lining a square or rectangular plastic box, loaf tin or casserole dish. When the food is frozen, lift the bag out of container and stack the blocks. Square or rectangular packages take up much less space than round ones. Slim, flat, evenly packed bags of frozen vegetables, cooked rice or pasta will not only make good use of space but will also defrost more quickly than bulky or spherical ones, especially if you are using a microwave. You may also find it helpful to split bulky items into smaller packages, especially in an upright freezer.

Use each shelf in an upright freezer for different foods, eg all the meat together, frozen fruit and vegetables together, etc. In a chest freezer this can be more difficult, so coloured plastic bags or small stacking baskets can help to organise foods, while rigid plastic boxes can help to protect more fragile foods.

What's in a name

Label foods clearly: there is nothing more frustrating than trying to guess the contents of an ice block, and defrosting it thinking it is a chicken casserole only to discover it is stewed apples! If you can, try to keep a record book so that you know exactly what is in the freezer. Failing that, rotate foods regularly and use up the oldest items first. Although foods will not go 'off' if frozen for longer times than recommended, you may find that the flavour and texture have been impaired.

Keeping cold

A freezer maintains low temperatures by conduction, so large spaces warm up quickly making the freezer work harder so using more electricity. Fill up spaces cheaply with bread or frozen vegetables; even clean newspapers will do.

Check the temperature and adjust to the recommended – 18°C. A freezer should never be allowed to be warmer than this for safety reasons, while keeping foods colder has no added advantage and of course means that the freezer will be using more electricity than needed.

Positioning of the freezer can also cause it to work harder. Try to make sure that the freezer is in a cool, dry place with adequate space behind and at the top or sides for the air to circulate around the vents.

Try to avoid opening the freezer unnecessarily and close the door as quickly as possible. It will take at least 30 minutes for the freezer to return to its original temperature again.

Freezer management – defrosting the freezer

This must be one of those jobs we all put off unless you are lucky enough to own a frost free freezer. As a guide, an upright freezer should really be defrosted three or four times a year, a chest freezer once or twice a year. Upright freezers need defrosting more regularly as they lose more cold air than a chest freezer each time the door is opened.

Try to defrost when the freezer is running low and you have two to three hours spare. If you have some freezer blocks then it is a good idea to freeze these down the night before.

Take the food out of the deep freeze, sort out the contents as quickly as possible into foods that you want to keep – put these in black bin bags, in compact blocks so that foods will not defrost, then wrap them in a sheet or newspapers then towels or a thick blacket for maximum insulation. Or put as much as you can into the fridge, and the remainder into picnic boxes with ice blocks. Put the items you are not sure about to one side.

Turn off the deep freeze, take out the bung from the base of a chest freezer, or flip out the defrosting spout at the base of an upright freezer. Line the base of a chest freezer with a pile of newspapers, or put a pile of newspapers in the base of an upright freezer with a few just tucked under the door. Half fill roasting tins, washing up bowls, etc with hot water and put them into the freezer to speed up defrosting, leaving the door open. Meanwhile sort through those unidentifiable bags and boxes, defrost the oldest or put them into a bag, ready to go back into the freezer. Aim to use these up within the next few weeks. Keep food as cold as possible.

Lift off ice from the newspaper before it has a chance to melt. Scrape off any ice from the inside of the freezer, and put more boiling water into the containers. Continue loosening ice with a plastic spatula or scraper and replacing the water until the freezer has defrosted.

Wash the inside of the freezer well with a bowl of water containing washing up liquid. If strong smells persist, wipe the inside with an odourless cleaner or bicarbonate of soda dissolved in water, then dry it well. Turn the freezer back on to fast freeze. Wash and dry the baskets, reload the freezer after 30 minutes. Switch it back to the normal freezer setting after 3 hours.

3 Freezer safety

Back to basics

Freezing is the simplest, most natural way to preserve foods as the food poisioning bacteria will not multiply at very low temperatures. A freezer works on the same principle as a fridge, but the refrigerant is at a higher pressure and the evaporator and heat exchanger are bigger, making it possible to achieve very low temperatures.

Most foods are made up largely of water, and as the food begins to freeze so the water in each cell changes to ice. The slower the food is frozen the larger the ice crystals and the larger the ice crystals the greater the chance that the crystals will puncture the cell wall and cause the food to loose nutrients and structure on defrosting. The most obvious example of this is seen when freezing strawberries: they completely collapse when defrosted. For best results freeze them in puréed form. Surprisingly, even lean meat contains 70 per cent water.

Preparing food for the freezer

Food hygiene is obviously vitally important, but even more so when preparing foods for the elderly whose resistance to infection may be lowered.

- Wash hands and clean work surfaces before cooking.
- Change dish cloths, tea towels etc frequently.
- Always wash knives, chopping boards and equipment between handling raw and cooked foods to avoid cross contamination.
- Make sure any raw foods taken from the freezer are thoroughly defrosted before use.
- Never refreeze food unless it is taken out of freezer 'raw' and returned to the freezer 'cooked and cooled'.

- Cool cooked foods quickly and always make sure foods are covered.

Cool foods quickly

Transfer cooked food to a cold container, cover it and stand it in a sink or washing up bowl, half filled with cold water. Stir occasionally to help reduce temperature. Transfer the food to the fridge as soon as possible. Pack it into freezer dishes when it is cold. Cover with a lid, foil or cling film immediately, label and pack into the freezer.

Batch baking

When batch cooking for the freezer it is important never to freeze more than one-tenth of your freezer's capacity in any 24 hours.

If you add more than this, you will push up the temperature inside the freezer, so causing the freezer to work harder, freeze the food slowly and possibly affect the food already in the freezer. While a temperature of −18°C is right for the storage of frozen foods, a lower temperature of −28°C is necessary for freezing fresh food. This lower temperature can be achieved by switching the freezer to fast freeze several hours in advance. Some foods have a fast freeze compartment which helps to isolate the 'new' food you are adding to the freezer.

For small amounts, up to 2 lb (1 kg), simply put food in the coldest part of the freezer, at the bottom of a chest freezer and towards the back of an upright freezer, and leave the freezer on its usual setting.

Star quality

Although we are all used to the idea of freezing home cooked foods and buying ready frozen foods, many people still get confused about the use of a freezer compartment in the fridge. This must not be used for freezing raw foods and is only suitable for ready frozen products. These foods all carry a star rating on the label as a guide to storage times.

*   –6°C will store frozen food for 1 week
**   –12°C will store frozen food for 1 month
*** –18°C will store frozen food for 3 months
* *** this four star marking shows a single star and then three stars banded together. It is an international symbol which distinguishes a genuine freezer from a cabinet which can only store frozen food

To check the temperature of the ice compartment in your fridge and freezer, use a freezer thermometer; these are available from good hardware shops.

Buying frozen foods

Make sure you buy frozen foods at the very end of a shopping trip. Pack them into a cool bag preferably with a frozen ice block and take the food home as quickly as possible for minimum defrosting.

Freezer reminders

- Make sure that the freezer is kept at –18°C.
- Wrap and label foods clearly.
- Keep the freezer as full as possible.
- Rotate foods and use the oldest first.
- Defrost a chest freezer once or twice a year, and an upright three or four times a year.
- Double check that the freezer door is tightly closed after opening.
- Tape over the plug so that the freezer cannot be turned off accidentally.

Never

- fill a chest freezer above the load line
- refreeze food that has been frozen before
- freeze liquid filled bottles or cans of fizzy drink as they may burst
- put hot food into a freezer

- add more than 10 per cent unfrozen food to freezer at any one time.

FREEZER STORAGE TIMES

MEAT AND POULTRY

Beef and lamb	4–6 months
Minced beef	3–4 months
Pork and veal	4–6 months
Sausages and sausagemeat	2–3 months
Offal	3–4 months
Ham and bacon joints	3–4 months
Chicken and turkey	10–12 months
Duck and goose	4–6 months
Venison	10–12 months
Rabbit and hare	4–6 months

FISH

White fish	6–8 months
Oily fish	3–4 months
Fish portions	3–4 months
Shellfish	2–3 months

FRUIT AND VEGETABLES

Fruit either with or without sugar	8–10 months
Fruit juices	4–6 months
Most vegetables	10–12 months
Mushrooms and tomatoes	6–8 months
Vegetable purées	6–8 months

DAIRY PRODUCE

Cream	6–8 months
Butter – unsalted	6–8 months
Butter – salted	3–4 months
Cheese – hard	4–6 months
Cheese – soft	3–4 months
Ice cream and similar products	3–4 months

PREPARED FOODS

Ready prepared meals – highly seasoned	2–3 months
Ready prepared meals – average seasoning	4–6 months
Boil in bag meals	4–6 months
Cakes	4-6 months
Bread – all kinds	2–3 months
Sandwiches	2–3 months
Bread dough	2–3 months
Other yeast products and pastries	3–4 months

Times compiled by the Food Safety Advisory Centre

Defrosting do's and don'ts

Although the bacteria that cause food poisoning cannot multiply in or on frozen food, they can soon develop on defrosting or on defrosted food in the same way as any other perishable food. Many elderly people may have reduced resistance to such infections and so it is worth running over this basic checklist, although most will be second nature to any experienced cook.

Do

- Defrost foods in the bottom of the fridge whenever possible, so that the ice crystals break down slowly, ensuring that they do not rupture the cell walls and affect the texture of the food.

- Defrost large solid items in a cool airy place, and drain and transfer them to the fridge as soon as possible.
- Defrost items on a dish or metal tray, anything washable and large enough to collect the drips.
- Avoid overcrowding as this will increase defrosting time.
- Keep foods loosely wrapped to shield them from any bacteria in the air.
- Allow plenty of time – defrosting always takes longer than you expect.
- Cook all vegetables, except corn on the cob, straight from the freezer.
- Follow manufacturers' guidelines for defrosting in a microwave.

For meat, fish and poultry:

- Defrost small cuts of meat in the fridge for 24 hours; 36–48 hours for larger cuts.
- Check poultry carefully before cooking – look inside the body cavity: there should be no ice crystals; legs should be soft and flexible. Meat and poultry should be completely defrosted before cooking.
- Cook small cuts of fish straight from the freezer. Larger fish should be defrosted before cooking, so too should shellfish or anything with an ice glaze.

Don't

- Do not try to speed up thawing by putting foods in hot water, eg the Christmas turkey! In an emergency submerge wrapped food in a bowl of cold water and change the water frequently.

GUIDE TO DEFROSTING TIMES

	Thawing in a refrigerator	Thawing at a cool room temperature	Thawing in a microwave
MEAT			
Joints over 1.5 kg (3.3 lb)	6–7 hours per 450 g	2–3 hours per 450 g	9–12 min per 450 g
Joints under 1.5 kg	3–4 hours per 450 g	1–2 hours per 450 g	9–12 min per 450 g
Steak or chops 2.5 cm (1 inch) thick	5–6 hours	2–4 hours	6–10 min per chop or steak
POULTRY			
Birds 3 kg (6.6 lb)	Minimum of 24 hours 5–8 hours per 450 g	Minimum of 9 hours 2½–3½ hours per 450 g	9–12 min per 450 g
Birds under 3 kg (6.6 lb)	Minimum of 24 hours	Minimum of 9 hours	9–12 min per 450 g
Poultry portions	6–8 hours	Not recommended	6–10 min per portion
FISH			
Whole fish or thick portions	4–5 hours per 450 g	1–2 hours per 450 g	5 min per 450 g
Fillets or thin flat fish	3–4 hours per 450 g or cook from frozen	1–2 hours per 450 g or cook from frozen	5 min per 450 g or cook from frozen
VEGETABLES	Cook from frozen		
PREPARED MEALS	Follow manufacturers instructions		

Compiled by the Food Safety Advisory Centre. 450 g = 1 lb

Foods that may be cooked from frozen:

frozen vegetables — except corn on the cob
frozen fish fillets
grated cheddar cheese
breadcrumbs, sliced bread
crumble mixture
frozen fruit.

Microwave magic

More than half of British homes now have a freezer and a microwave. A freezer and microwave can prove to be the perfect partnership for speedy defrosting and reheating. For those living on their own a microwave can also save on fuel – why heat up a large oven just to reheat one portion of food. But, although it can save money on a day to day basis, the initial cost of a microwave must be borne in mind.

When buying a microwave for an elderly person try to choose a basic easy to operate model with a clear, easy to read timer. A basic model will not only be cheaper but less complicated to operate. Digital controls are the easiest to read and by far the best and most precise for short cooking times. They may, though, take a little getting used to.

Microwaves are available in different wattages, although 650 and 700 watt models are the most commonly sold. If your model has a lower power output than this then you will need to increase the timings in all the recipes. See your microwave handbook for more details about adjusting timings.

Defrosting tips

- Set the temperature control to defrost or 30 per cent – some microwaves only have numbers for power. Set for the time specified in recipe or see the table below for guidelines.

- Always remove plastic covered metal tags from plastic bags or these will cause sparks or arcing when the microwave is turned on.

- If food is in a plastic bag then stand this in a serving dish to catch any drips. Remove the bag towards the end of cooking and use it to cover the food.

- Make sure serving dishes or plates do not have any metal rims or gold or silver patterns since these will go black with microwaving.

- If frozen food is in a metal or foil container then remove it before defrosting. To remove the dish easily, turn the dish upside down, rinse it with hot water then lift off.

- Check plastic containers during defrosting and reheating. They can distort as food heats up, so transfer food to a serving dish as soon as possible.

- If raw food begins to cook during defrosting then turn the power off. Leave the food to stand for 10–15 minutes so that the temperature can equalise before microwaving again.

Reheating reminders

- Make sure that food is thoroughly reheated to at least 70°C for at least 2 minutes, so that any harmful bacteria that could cause food poisoning are killed.

- To make double sure, test with a food thermometer.

- Cooking times on food labels or in cookery books should not be shortened unless you are using a fan assisted oven. Follow the handbook for guidelines, but as a rule reduce temperatures by 10°C or times by 10 minutes for each hour of cooking.

- Only reheat food once.

When using a microwave:

- Always cover food with a plate or pierced cling film so that food does not dry out.

- For plated meals try to arrange the denser foods around the edge of the plate. More delicate, less dense foods should be in the centre as these will heat up more slowly.

- Put pastries and bread on a sheet of kitchen paper so that they do not go soggy.

- Reheat sliced meats with a few spoonfuls of gravy so that it does not dry out.

- For large quantities always stir before serving and allow the food to stand for 5 minutes so that any hot spots can equalise.

- Always check that the food is thoroughly reheated before serving. Cook it a little longer if needed.

- If reheating more than one item, remember to increase the cooking time.

SOS – what to do if the freezer is accidently turned off

If the freezer is three-quarters full or more, the food should stay frozen hard for a minimum of 12 hours, providing of course that the lid or door is unopened.

If the freezer has only been turned off for a short while, check the food first. If it is still hard and frosty then quickly turn the freezer back on to fast freeze and leave it for at least 3 hours. Return the freezer to normal temperature and avoid opening the door for as long as possible.

If the freezer has been turned off overnight then once again check the food. If meat and fish, cooked dishes and dairy foods are still hard, then turn the freezer back on to fast freeze immediately. Quickly remove ice creams, frozen vegetables and fruit. Shellfish will need thorough defrosting and will have to be eaten immediately. Ice cream will have to be thrown away. Fruit can be made into jam, but add 10 per cent extra to your usual recipe; for smaller amounts, cook the fruit and make it into pies and crumbles. Make vegetables into soups and casseroles then cool and return them in cooked form to the freezer. Bread, biscuits, plain cakes and uncooked pastry (without eggs) can be refrozen – these are the only exceptions.

If meat and fish products have defrosted then these will need cooking and cooling before they can be returned to the freezer. If anything has a strong, unpleasant odour or looks bloody, then get rid of it at once. If in any doubt about any item of food throw it out: this is far better than giving everyone an upset tummy.

Should the freezer be turned off accidentally when going on holiday then transfer all foods to large bin bags, seal well and take them straight down to the local amenity tip. Keep a record as you sort out so that you can make an insurance claim on your household insurance policy. The insurance company will not want to see the food as proof.

If you discover that your freezer door has been left open, again check the food inside. In most cases the freezer will still be functioning, although working exceptionally hard to maintain the temperature. You will probably find a large build up of ice around the door, making it incredibly difficult to shut. Try to chip off the ice with a scraper, plastic spatula or wooden spoon. Shut the door as soon as you can, turn the freezer on to fast freeze and leave it for three hours.

If the freezer needs defrosting so that you can shut the door then ring round friends and neighbours and see if they can store the most perishable foods in their freezers. Large joints or frozen cooked casseroles – food in large blocks – should not defrost too quickly and can be wrapped in a blanket or newspapers to keep cold. Speed up defrosting of the empty icy freezer with roasting tins and washing up bowls of boiling water, see p.10.

Power cuts

If you have a power cut, avoid opening the freezer door. If left undisturbed a freezer will not start to defrost, providing it is well stocked, for at least 12 hours. Increase the insulation by wrapping the freezer with thick blankets or a duvet.

Ring the electricity board and check the seriousness of the fault. If it is an extended local power cut, perhaps as the result of a storm, it may be worth sharing the cost of hiring a small generator between your neighbours and using it in two hourly shifts until the power is resumed.

Check the food as soon as the power is back on. If it is still frozen solid then turn freezer to fast freeze and leave it undisturbed. If food has begun to defrost proceed as previous page.

Faulty freezer

Check the obvious: perhaps the mains switch has been turned off or a child has fiddled with the switches. It may be a faulty thermostat or more seriously a faulty compressor. Check your guarantee or service agreement then get in touch immediately with the maintenance or service department. See your instruction booklet or look in Yellow Pages for telephone numbers. If it seems that an engineer cannot get to you for some time leave the freezer unopened. If it is only half full, then fill up any empty space in the freezer with crumpled news-paper – this should be the only time that the freezer is opened until repairs can be made. Insulate the outside of the freezer with blankets, rugs or sacks. As soon as the freezer is fixed, quickly check the state of the food inside. See previous page for what to do next.

Will I be covered by insurance?

Most household insurance policies will automatically cover the loss of food from a freezer. Some policies require you to specify a freezer in the list of contents while others do not. Amounts covered also vary from £250–500 with most carrying an excess of £50, ie: you cannot claim for the first £50 of food lost.

An 'all risks' policy will cover accidental damage, should the freezer be turned off by mistake, while other policies may only cover food lost through a power cut. The insurance company will not expect you to keep the food but will expect an itemised list written out on a claim form. As with all insurance policies it is wise to read the small print, especially if buying a freezer for the first time, so that you are prepared in advance should a disaster strike.

CFCs

There's been a lot of media coverage about CFCs – chlorofluorocarbons – the gases thought to be responsible for the thinning of the ozone layer. Although a new alternative has yet to be found, some manufacturers now produce fridges, fridge/freezers and freezers which have a 50 per cent reduction of CFCs in their system. A few major stores will also remove your old freezer and dispose of the CFC gas safely and recyle as many parts of the old freezer as they can. This is certainly a good step in the right direction.

4 Getting organised

Basic equipment

There is no need to spend out on expensive cooking equipment. The most essential item to have is a large saucepan. Get that preserving pan out from the back of the cupboard, give it a good wash and use it to make soups and stews. They seldom come with a lid so improvise with a large baking sheet or foil.

Alternatively, if you have a pressure cooker, then use the base for frying and cooking. If you need a lid then use it as a normal pan lid without the weights.

A large flameproof casserole, that can be used on the hob and in the oven, is useful but can be an expensive purchase. While large casserole dishes can be cheaper, a large turkey roasting tin works just as well, covered tightly with foil. Check out your local car boot sales; it is always amazing to see the mixture of items for sale and you may be able to pick up some large dishes quite cheaply.

In the recipes, a food processor, liquidiser and electric mixer have been mentioned where appropriate. These are expensive items and while not essential can save much time and effort. So do use them to the full if you own them already.

A food processor is probably the most versatile gadget to own as it can chop, purée, beat and, with the easy addition of extra blades and discs, grate and slice. The catch – they cost anything between £40 and £100. A small hand held electric mixer can be bought for around £15 while a basic liquidiser costs around £20.

Portion control

Pack food in handy sized portions. All the recipes in this book have been packed into single portions, but do adjust this to suit your own family's needs. You may find it more useful to do a mix of portion sizes or to pack all single portions into one large bag so that they are easy to locate in the freezer.

When freezing chops or slices of cake it is a good idea to inter-leave them with freezer tissue, small pieces of foil or cling film before packing them into a bag or box, so that single items can be removed for defrosting. If you intend to buy large packs of mince or sausages then divide them into smaller more useable sized portions before freezing.

Packing food into small parcels also means that loading the freezer is easier as shapes are more compact. Smaller portions will also defrost more quickly.

Packing up

There is a wide range of products available, some of which you may have in your kitchen already, such as foil, cling film and polythene bags – not only the most widely used but probably the cheapest too.

It is vitally important to wrap all foods going into the freezer. This is not a manufacturer's gimmick to get you to buy more packaging materials, but to keep the food in prime condition. As in a fridge, foodstuffs quickly dry out in the freezer. Wrapping in foil, polythene or cling film not only prevents this, but also stops the transference of smells and tastes from one food to another.

Make sure that whatever packaging materials you choose they:

- will act as a barrier against moisture and air
- will be greaseproof, so that any fat present will not work its way through the packaging before the food is frozen
- are odourless with no smell or taste of their own
- must be thin enough not to take up valuable freezer space
- must be tough enough to withstand knocks.

Foil

Heavy gauge foil is best for freezing, while ordinary kitchen foil should be used double thickness. Wash and reuse foil after freezing for cooking purposes. Flexible and strong, foil is good for wrapping awkward shaped items such as joints of meat or chops, but do be careful that the bones don't puncture the foil. Make sure to press out any air between food and foil and to seal edges well.

A wide range of foil dishes are also available from most large supermarkets. Avoid using these for fruit or foods with a high acid or vinegar content as this may cause pitting. Washed carefully these containers can be used several times, although the lids will need replacing with a piece of foil. Make sure to seal the edges well.

Cling film

Cling film is very flexible and strong; use freezer gauge film for extra protection. Good visibility means foods are easy to identify. Press out any air between food and film and seal ends well. Make sure that cling film does not come into direct contact with fatty foods, and do not use it to wrap cheese or butter.

Polythene bags

It is best to buy bags marked 'freezer bags' for extra strength, since the thinner ones tend to tear easily. They are available in a huge range of sizes. Try to pack items as squarely and flatly as possible for best use of the freezer.

Boil in the bags

These special heavy duty polythene bags can be used for freezing food and then later for reheating by cooking in a saucepan of boiling water. Although they are useful they can be expensive and difficult to buy.

Plastic containers

Recycle plastic yogurt pots, cottage cheese pots with lids, margarine and ice cream tubs. Although not as strong or long lasting as purpose made Tupperware they make great freebie containers. If you plan to freeze large cakes it may be worthwhile buying one or two plastic containers of the right size. Pack the cake on the lid then cover it with the base. Mark the top clearly so that you know the contents are fragile.

Recycle plastic containers from ready meals too. Cut the meals into single dishes if appropriate. Use the containers to freeze foods and reheat foods, but make sure that dishes are not reheated above 350°F, 180°C, Gas 4, or they will melt.

China and glass containers

There are a wide range of dishes available. It is best to choose oven-proof china or Pyrex dishes for greater flexibility. Never freeze fine china or glass and never freeze bottles as they may explode. Always overwrap dishes if there isn't a lid, using foil or cling film.

It is best to freeze foods for short times or you may run out of dishes. Alternatively, line dishes with foil or cling film, add food, freeze until solid then remove the dish. Overwrap the block, label it and freeze. Return the block to the dish for defrosting and cooking but remember to remove foil or cling film first.

Where to buy

Most of the above items are available from your local supermarket, specialist freezer shop or by mail order from Lakeland Plastics. Ring 015394 88100 for a catalogue packed with reasonably priced, practical cooking and freezing aids.

Look out for china and Pyrex dishes from jumble sales, car boot sales, end of season or closing down sales in shops.

Open-freezing

Protect very fragile foods such as cakes, pies and decorated puddings by open-freezing them until they are solid. Freeze the food unwrapped, on a small baking sheet, plate or lid of a plastic box until it is just solid. Remove and overwrap with cling film or a plastic box base. For a pie, overwrap it with cling film and pack it into a plastic box for added protection then return to freezer.

Free flow bags

For tiny items such as peas, sliced vegetables, red and black currants and raspberries, freeze foods in a single layer on a large baking sheet. When hard, transfer the food to a plastic bag. Freezing in this way ensures that the food does not stick together, enabling you to take just the amount out of the bag that you require.

Dry sugar pack

This is the most suitable method for freezing soft, juicy fruits. The quantity of sugar varies, depending on the sweetness of the fruit, but as a guide use 4–6 oz (100–150 g) sugar per 1 lb (450 g) of fruit. Coat the whole or sliced fruit in sugar or pack into plastic boxes with alternate layers of fruit and sugar. Leave ½ inch (1cm) of headspace, cover, seal, label and freeze. Defrost in the fridge or at room temperature and use just before the fruit has completely defrosted.

Syrup pack

This is the best method for freezing hard, non-juicy fruits which discolour quickly, eg peaches, apricots, plums and pears. Make the syrup by dissolving three cups of granulated sugar in four cups of water. Cool the liquid and pour it into a plastic box.

Peel and stone the fruit if needed then slice it directly into the syrup to help prevent discolouration. Make sure that the syrup completely covers the fruit and leave ½ inch (1 cm) headspace. Cover, seal and label.

The importance of sealing

It is vitally important to seal all containers well, not only to avoid spills but to also prevent food from drying out.

For solid foods, suck out as much air as possible from plastic bags with a straw or by simply squeezing air out with hands. Seal with a plastic covered wire tie or a clothes peg. Making the package as air free as possible helps to prevent discolouration and freezer burn and also makes it more compact.

However, for liquids it is important to leave some air or headspace to allow for expansion once the soup or sauce has frozen. As a rough guide allow ½ inch for each ½ pint of liquid.

Labelling

It's all too easy to skip the label and then spend frustrating moments in the months ahead trying to detect the contents of that frosted bag. There's nothing worse than defrosting something that you thought was savoury only to discover it's sweet!

Labels come in a wide range of sizes and colours. Some freezer bags come with a white write-on panel, or look out for tie write tags, a combined tie and label in one. Make sure that the pen you are using will not run or smudge in the freezer. Special freezer pens are available but a cheap biro is perfectly adequate.

Always write on the label the number of servings, the date it went into the freezer or if preferred the date the food should be used by.

If cooking for someone else then buy larger labels and write on defrosting and reheating instructions to save any confusion.

What is freezer burn

This is most commonly found on meat, poultry and fish and is usually caused by dehydration, resulting from poor or torn packaging. The greyish-white patches are harmless but cause the food to taste spongy and rather unpleasant. Remove the affected areas once the food has defrosted or throw the food away if freezer burn is too extensive.

Quick tips

- Do not pack foods with a high acid content such as rhubarb, gooseberries and apples, or savoury dishes with vinegar or wine, into foil dishes since the acid can cause 'pitting'.

- Do not put hot foods into plastic or waxed containers as they will melt.

- Do not let unfrozen foods come into contact with frozen food in the freezer. Make sure items are well wrapped. Don't forget to label them.

- Thickened liquids tend to become thicker once they have been frozen.

- Seasonings can taste stronger on thawing.

- The more you can cool the food before putting it into the freezer the better.

Making an ice bowl

Surprisingly cheap and easy to make, an ice bowl can make a pretty centrepiece to a summer or winter party filled with scoops of ice cream or as an extra special wine cooler.

Find two plastic or glass mixing bowls so that one will fit inside the other, leaving a gap of about ¾–1 inch (2–2.5 cm). Double check that bowls will fit into the freezer, then remove and pour a little cold water into the base of the larger bowl. Tape across the two bowls with two long pieces of freezer tape to secure. Put the bowls on a plate to catch any water drips.

Now choose a selection of decorations, sprigs of fresh herbs and edible flowers such as pansies, marigolds and borage from the garden, lemon geranium leaves, sliced lemons, limes and oranges, or sliced strawberries, strings of black and red currants, or whole raspberries. For a festive version, you can use bay leaves and cranberries arranged like holly, sliced oranges and a few whole spices such as cloves, star anise or pieces of cinnamon stick.

Insert the decorations into the water in the large bowl. When you are happy with the arrangement transfer the bowls to the freezer and freeze overnight until solid. If you find the decorations keep floating then pour out some of the water, freeze the half filled bowl until solid then complete as above.

Take the bowls out of the freezer. Remove the plate and dip the bowls into a washing up bowl half filled with boiling water. Count to 15 then remove it. Peel away the tape, prise a knife between the large bowl and the ice to release the air. Turn the bowls upside down and remove the large bowl.

Turn the ice bowl back up the right way and pour a little hot water into the small bowl. Loosen the bowl with a knife then remove. Put the ice bowl back on the plate and freeze it until required.

5 How to use the recipes

Over the next pages you will find over 100 budget recipes to cover all meal situations from a quick lunch to a hearty main meal, and puddings, even tasty teatime treats, are included. All recipes are designed to be frozen in handy one portion packs, perfect for those living on their own, for elderly dependent relatives unable to cook for themselves or for families where members eat at different times.

The price is right

All recipes are marked with a £ symbol to indicate price.

£   for portions under 25p
££   for portions between 25p and 50p
£££ for portions between 50p and 85p

Just under 50 of the recipes in the book can be made for 25p or under, 36 cost between 25p and 50p and the remainder, which include many meaty main courses, cost under 85p a portion.

The prices have all been calculated on supermarket prices in June 1995. Prices may of course vary, depending on seasons, national availablility and special offer bargains from street markets or freezer centres. Look out for the additional shopping tips at the end of each recipe to help reduce prices even more.

Measure for measure

All recipes carry imperial and metric measurements; please use just one of these and not a combination of the two. All spoon measures are level and have been tested using a plastic set of measuring spoons of the type available from cook shops and hardware stores. If using

33

your own household spoons remember these may vary considerably, particularly when using tablespoons.

Adapting the recipes

Each recipe is illustrated with easy to read symbols and helpful tips, highlighting recipes that are quick to cook, use store cupboard ingredients or give suggestions for interchanging ingredients and cooking methods, plus of course valuable freezing notes.

Do interchange ingredients where appropriate or where a cheaper alternative is available. Use fresh meat instead of frozen if it is cheaper or on special offer. Use fresh herbs if you have them in the garden; avoid expensive fresh herbs from the supermarket. Dried herbs are perfectly acceptable and have a long storage life. Interchange spices if you find you've run out of one. Large tubs of budget priced soft margarine have been used for most recipes, but add butter if you'd rather and can afford it.

Freeze ahead

All recipes can be successfully frozen in one portion packs. Each recipe carries instructions on how to serve the recipe immediately, how to pack and store it in the freezer, plus comprehensive defrosting instructions with or without a microwave.

Key to the recipe symbols

Price per portion:

£

Under 25p

£ £

Between 25
and 50p

£ £ £

Between 50
and 85p

Shopping tip

Suitabe for a vegetarian

Freezer tip

Nutritional information

Uses store cupboard
ingredients

Cooking method

· Expert tip

Ingredients tip

Serving suggestion

Recipe that is quick
to cook

SOUP AND A SNACK

Bacon and potato soup

Gingered carrot and butter bean soup

Turkey broth

Mushroom and thyme soup

Spiced dahl soup

Minestrone soup

Lamb hotchpotch

Cream of broccoli soup

Tomato and lentil broth

Leek and bacon chowder

Quick snacks

Cheese and chive scones

Sausages in blankets

Cheese and onion toasties

Pesto pizzas

Spicy beef pockets

Freezeable sandwiches

Bacon and potato soup

Uses store cupboard
ingredients.

Ingredients tip Avoid highly
seasoned Oxo style stock
cubes. Sprinkle with a little
parsley from the garden or
freezer just before serving.

Expert tip Frying the onions
slowly brings out the flavour.

Freezing tip Soup may be
defrosted by heating gently in
a saucepan for 15 minutes,
boil for 3 minutes, stirring.

Serves 8   Cost £

4 rashers streaky bacon

4 medium onions

2 oz (50 g) soft margarine

1½ lb (675 g) potatoes

2pt (1.1 litre) chicken stock

1 Cut rind away from bacon and then chop. Chop onions.

2 Heat margarine in a large saucepan, add bacon and onions and fry gently for 10 minutes, stirring occasionally until golden.

3 Peel and chop potatoes. Add to pan and fry for 2–3 minutes. Pour on stock and season well with salt and pepper.

4 Bring soup to the boil then cover and simmer for 30 minutes.

5 Purée three ladles of soup in a food processor or liquidiser then stir back into soup.

To serve now: *reheat then ladle into bowls.*

To freeze: *cool completely then pack portions into small plastic bags. Seal, label and freeze for 4–6 months.*

To defrost: *put as many portions as required into a saucepan, still in bags. Defrost for 4 hours at room temperature. Remove bags, boil for 3 minutes, stirring.*

To microwave: *remove metal tag and microwave bag in a microproof serving bowl on full power for 3 minutes. Remove bag, stir and cook for 2 minutes more. Stir just before serving*

37

Gingered carrot and butter bean soup

Vegetarian tip Use vegetable stock.

Ingredients tip Omit ginger if preferred. Use homemade chicken stock or a mild stock cube, avoid Oxo style cubes.

Freezing tip Defrost frozen soup by gently heating in a saucepan for 15 minutes. Boil for 3 minutes. Add a little extra water or stock if needed.

Serves 8   Cost £

1 onion

1¾ lb (800 g) carrots

1 oz (25 g) soft margarine

15 oz (420 g) can butter beans

1 tsp ground ginger

2 pt (1.1 litre) chicken stock

½ pt (300 ml) milk

1   Peel and chop onion and carrots. Heat margarine in a large saucepan and fry vegetables gently, stirring occasionally for 10 minutes until lightly browned.

2   Drain butter beans and add to pan with ginger, stock and plenty of salt and pepper. Bring to the boil, cover and simmer for 30 minutes.

3   Purée soup in a food processor or liquidiser in small batches and then return to pan. Stir in milk.

To serve now: *reheat soup and ladle into dishes. Serve with Sausages in blankets, see p.49.*

To freeze: *cool completely then ladle portions into small plastic bags. Seal, label and freeze for 4–6 months.*

To defrost: *put as many portions as required into a saucepan, still in bags. Defrost for 4 hours at room temperature. Remove bags, boil for 3 minutes, stirring.*

To microwave: *remove metal tag and microwave bag in a microproof serving bowl on full power for 3 minutes. Remove bag, stir and cook for 2 minutes more. Stir just before serving.*

Turkey broth

Shopping tip Look out for bags of soup mix alongside the lentils and dried pulses in the supermarket.

Ingredients tip Turkey drumsticks are surprisingly cheap at only 99p each.

Cooking method If you don't have a saucepan big enough then put turkey into a roasting tin and cover tightly with foil, cook on hob as recipe.

Serving tip A hearty meal in a bowl.

Serves 8   Cost £

9 oz (250 g) pkt country soup mix, soaked overnight in cold water

1 turkey drumstick

bunch fresh herbs or 1 tsp dried mixed herbs

1 onion

8 oz (225 g) carrots

12 oz (350 g) swede

1 tbsp oil

2 pt (1.1 litre) chicken stock

3 tsp wholegrain mustard

---

1 Drain soup mix and set aside.

2 Rinse turkey drumstick with cold water and put into a large saucepan with 2 pt (1.1 litre) water, herbs and salt and pepper. Cover and simmer for 1 hour.

3 Peel and chop onion, carrot and swede.

4 Take turkey out of pan, strain stock into a jug and then heat oil in pan. Add onion and fry for 5 minutes, stirring occasionally until softened.

5 Add carrot and swede and fry for 2–3 minutes.

6 Take turkey meat off bone discarding skin and gristle. Finely chop and add to soup with drained soup mix, turkey stock, chicken stock, mustard and plenty of salt and pepper.

7 Bring to the boil and boil rapidly for 10 minutes. Reduce heat and simmer for 45 minutes, stirring occasionally.

39

To serve now: *ladle into large bowls and serve with crusty bread.*

To freeze: *cool completely. Pack portions into small plastic bags. Seal, label and freeze for 4–6 months.*

To defrost: *put as many portions as required into a saucepan, still in bags. Defrost for 4 hours at room temperature. Remove bag, boil for 5 minutes, stirring.*

To microwave: *remove metal tag and microwave bag in a microproof serving bowl on defrost (30 percent) for 10 minutes. Remove bag, stir and cook on full power for 3 minutes. Stir just before serving.*

Mushroom and thyme soup

Shopping tip A good way to use up bargain bulk buys of mushrooms from the market.

Vegetarian tip Use a vegetable stock cube.

Serving tip This soup is very dark, garnish with a

Serves 8   Cost ££

2 onions

2 oz (50 g) soft margarine

1 lb (450 g) potatoes

1 lb (450 g) cup mushrooms

1 lemon, grated rind and juice

2½ pt (1.5 litres) chicken stock

small bunch fresh thyme or 1 tsp dried

1 pt (600 ml) milk

---

1 Roughly chop onions. Heat margarine in a large saucepan and fry onions until softened and lightly browned.

2 Peel and chop potatoes. Wipe and chop mushrooms. Add to pan and fry for 3–4 minutes, stirring occasionally.

3 Stir in lemon rind and juice, stock and thyme. Season well with salt and pepper.

4 Bring to the boil then cover and simmer for 25 minutes.

little frozen parsley just before serving, if available.

Freezing tip If serving several portions, defrost for 4 hours at room temperature, in a covered saucepan, then boil for 3 minutes.

5 Discard fresh thyme stalks. Cool slightly then purée in batches in a liquidiser or food processor. Return to saucepan and stir in milk.

To serve now: reheat then ladle into bowls. Serve with Cheese and onion toasties, p.50.

To freeze: cool completely then pack portions into small plastic bags. Seal, label and freeze for 4–6 months.

To defrost: take portion out of bag, put in a saucepan, cover and reheat gently for 15 minutes, stirring occasionally. Boil for 3 minutes, stirring.

To microwave: remove metal tag and microwave bag in a microproof bowl on full power for 4 minutes. Remove bag, stir and cook for 2 minutes more. Stir just before serving.

Spiced dahl soup

Vegetarian tip Use vegetable stock.

Method tip If you don't have a liquidiser or food processor then leave soup chunky or break down with a potato masher.

Serves 8   Costs £

8 oz (225 g) yellow split peas, soaked overnight in cold water

2 onions

12 oz (350 g) parsnips

2 tbsp oil

4 cloves garlic, crushed

1½ tsp ground cumin

1½ tsp ground coriander

2 tsp turmeric

3 pt (1.7 litres) chicken stock

I Drain soaked peas and set aside.

2 Finely chop onions. Peel and chop parsnips. Heat oil in a large saucepan, fry onion and parsnips until softened and lightly browned.

41

3 Add garlic and spices and fry for 1 minute, stirring. Stir in stock and drained split peas. Season well with salt and pepper then bring mixture to the boil.

4 Cover and simmer for 45 minutes until peas are very soft.

5 Purée half the soup in a liquidiser or food processor until smooth then stir back into the remaining soup.

To serve now: *reheat and ladle into bowls.*

To freeze: *cool completely then pack portions into plastic bags. Seal, label and freeze for 2–3 months.*

To defrost: *put as many portions as required into a saucepan, still in bags. Defrost for 4 hours at room temperature. Remove bags, boil for 3 minutes, stirring.*

To microwave: *remove metal tag and microwave bag in a microproof serving bowl on full power for 4 minutes. Remove bag, stir and cook for 2 minutes more. Stir just before serving.*

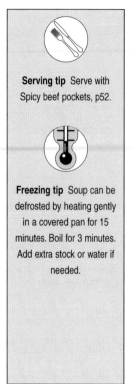

Serving tip Serve with Spicy beef pockets, p52.

Freezing tip Soup can be defrosted by heating gently in a covered pan for 15 minutes. Boil for 3 minutes. Add extra stock or water if needed.

Minestrone soup

Ingredients tip Don't have any small pasta shapes then break spaghetti into tiny pieces.

Serves 8   Costs £

2 onions

2 tbsp oil

1 lb (450 g) carrots

12 oz (350 g) courgettes

2 cloves garlic, crushed

14 oz (400 g) can tomatoes

3½ pt (2 litre) chicken stock

2 tsp caster sugar

2 oz (50 g) small pasta shapes

2 tbsp pesto sauce

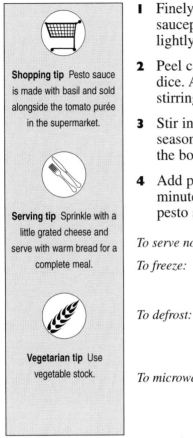

Shopping tip Pesto sauce is made with basil and sold alongside the tomato purée in the supermarket.

Serving tip Sprinkle with a little grated cheese and serve with warm bread for a complete meal.

Vegetarian tip Use vegetable stock.

I Finely chop onions. Heat oil in a large saucepan and fry onions until softened and lightly browned.

2 Peel carrots, trim courgettes, cut into small dice. Add to pan and fry for 3–4 minutes, stirring occasionally.

3 Stir in garlic, tomatoes, stock, sugar and season well with salt and pepper. Bring to the boil, cover and simmer for 15 minutes.

4 Add pasta and simmer, uncovered for 10 minutes or until pasta is cooked. Stir in pesto sauce.

To serve now: *ladle into bowls.*

To freeze: *cool completely then pack portions into plastic bags. Seal, label and freeze for 4–6 months.*

To defrost: *put as many portions as required into a saucepan, still in bags. Defrost for 4 hours at room temperature. Remove bags, boil for 3 minutes, stirring.*

To microwave: *remove metal tag and microwave bag in a microproof serving bowl on full power for 4 minutes. Remove bag, stir and cook for 2 minutes more. Stir just before serving.*

Lamb hotchpotch

Cooking tip Cook in a pressure cooker if preferred, see manual for timings.

Serves 8   Costs ££

2 lb (900 g) frozen neck (stewing) lamb, defrosted

2 onions

12 oz (350 g) swede

12 oz (350 g) carrot

12 oz (350 g) potato

3 pt (1.7 litre) chicken stock

small bunch fresh sage or 1 tsp dried

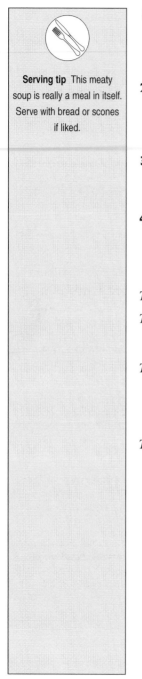

I Rinse lamb with cold water, drain well and dry with kitchen paper. Put into a large saucepan and dry fry lamb gently until fat begins to run.

2 Finely chop onions. Peel and dice root vegetables. Pile lamb up at one side of pan, add vegetables and fry for 5 minutes until softened.

3 Add stock, sage and season well with salt and pepper. Bring to the boil, cover and simmer for 1½ hours, stirring occasionally.

4 Lift meat out of pan, draining well. Cut meat away from bone with a knife and fork and discard fat. Cut meat into tiny pieces and return to pan.

To serve now: reheat and ladle into bowls.

To freeze: cool completely then pack portions into small plastic bags. Seal, label and freeze for 4–6 months.

To defrost: take out as many portions as required and put into a saucepan, still in bags. Defrost for 4 hours at room temperature. Remove bags, boil for 5 minutes, stirring.

To microwave: remove metal tag and microwave soup in bag in a microproof serving bowl on defrost (30 per cent) for 10 minutes. Remove bag, stir and cook on full power for 3 minutes. Stir just before serving.

Cream of broccoli soup

Shopping tip A good way to use up bargain buys of broccoli.

Ingredients tip Keep a handy supply of powdered milk in the cupboard: saves using your fresh milk supply for soups.

Cooking tip Don't overcook soup or colour will be very dark.

Serving tip Swirl in a little cream or yogurt, if available, just before serving

Vegetarian tip Use vegetable stock.

Serves 8   Costs £

2 onions

2 oz (50 g) soft margarine

2 heads of broccoli, about 1¾ lb (800 g)

2 pt (1.1 litre) chicken stock

1 pt (600 ml) milk

1   Chop onions. Heat margarine in a large saucepan, add onion and fry gently until softened and lightly browned.

2   Roughly chop broccoli florets and stems and add to pan. Fry for 2 minutes then pour on stock and season well with salt and pepper.

3   Bring to the boil, cover and simmer for 15 minutes until broccoli is tender and still bright green.

4   Cool slightly then purée in batches in a liquidiser or food processor. Return to saucepan and stir in milk.

To serve now: *reheat and ladle into bowls.*

To freeze: *cool completely then pack portions into small plastic bags. Seal, label and freeze for 1 month.*

To defrost: *put as many portions as required into a saucepan, still in bags. Defrost for 4 hours at room temperature. Remove bags, boil for 3 minutes, stirring.*

To microwave: *remove metal tag and microwave bag in a microproof serving bowl on full power for 3 minutes. Remove bag, stir and cook for 3 minutes more. Stir just before serving.*

45

Tomato and lentil broth

Uses store cupboard ingredients.

Vegetarian tip Use vegetable stock.

Cooking tip If you don't have a lid for your large pan then cover with a baking sheet.

Serves 8   Costs £

2 onions

2 tbsp oil

8 oz (225 g) potato

3 tsp paprika

½ tsp ground cinnamon

2 cloves garlic, crushed

6 oz (150 g) red lentils

2½ pt (1.5 litre) chicken stock

14 oz (400 g) can tomatoes

1 tsp caster sugar

I Finely chop onions. Heat oil in a large saucepan, add onions and fry until softened and lightly browned.

2 Peel and dice potato, add to pan with the paprika, cinnamon and garlic and fry for 2 minutes.

3 Stir in lentils, stock, tomatoes and sugar. Season well with salt and pepper. Bring to the boil, cover and simmer for 40 minutes or until lentils are soft.

To serve now: ladle into bowls.

To freeze: cool completely then pack portions into small plastic bags. Seal, label and freeze for 4–6 months.

To defrost: put as many portions as required into a saucepan, still in bags. Defrost for 4 hours at room temperature. Remove bags, boil for 3 minutes, stirring.

To microwave: remove metal tag and microwave bag in a microproof serving bowl on full power for 3 minutes. Remove bag, stir and cook for 3 minutes more. Stir just before serving.

Leek and bacon chowder

Quick to make.

Ingredients tip Use bacon offcuts if available to save money.

Cooking method Cut the potatoes into small pieces so that they cook quickly.

Freezing tip You may need to add a little extra milk when reheating soup.

Serves 8   Costs ££

2 onions

7 oz (200 g) streaky bacon

2 oz (50 g) soft margarine

2 lb (900 g) potatoes

2 pt (1.1 litre) milk

½ pt (300 ml) chicken stock

2 bay leaves

4 tsp whole grain mustard

12 oz (350 g) leeks

8 oz (225 g) frozen sweetcorn

I Finely chop onions. Cut rind away from bacon and then chop. Heat margarine in large saucepan, add onions and bacon and fry until just beginning to brown.

2 Peel and dice potatoes, add to pan with milk, stock, bay leaves and mustard. Season well with salt and pepper.

3 Bring to the boil, cover and simmer for 15 minutes.

4 Wash and thinly slice leeks. Add to pan with sweetcorn and cook, uncovered for 10 minutes or until vegetables are cooked.

To serve now: *ladle into bowls.*

To freeze: *cool completely then pack portions into small plastic bags. Seal, label and freeze for 1 month.*

To defrost: *put as many portions as required into a saucepan, still in bags. Defrost for 4 hours at room temperature. Remove bags, boil for 5 minutes, stirring.*

To microwave: *remove metal tag and microwave bag in a microproof serving bowl on defrost*

47

(30 per cent) for 10 minutes. Remove bag, stir and cook on full power for 2½ minutes. Stir just before serving.

QUICK SNACKS

Cheese and chive scones

Quick to cook Suitable for a vegetarian, check cheese label before using.

Ingredients tip Use chives from the garden or chopped green tops from a bunch of spring onions.

Expert tip Much quicker to cut into squares and saves rerolling dough.

Serves 8   Costs £

4 oz (100 g) block or soft margarine

1 lb (450 g) self-raising flour

6 oz (150 g) cheddar cheese, grated

4 tbsp fresh chopped chives

1 egg, size 3, beaten

6–7 fl oz (175–200 ml) milk

I Preheat the oven to 425°F, 220°C, Gas 7. Lightly grease a large baking sheet with a little of the margarine.

2 Put flour and a little salt and pepper into a bowl. Add margarine, cut into pieces and rub in with fingertips or an electric mixer until the mixture looks like fine breadcrumbs.

3 Stir in cheese and chives. Reserve 1 tbsp egg and 1 tbsp milk for glazing and mix remaining egg and milk into flour until a soft but not sticky dough.

4 Lightly knead and roll out on a floured surface until a rectangle 12 × 4 inch (30 × 10 cm). Cut into 16 pieces and put pieces, slightly spaced apart, on baking sheet.

5 Brush with reserved egg and milk and cook for 10–12 minutes until well risen and golden.

To serve now: *serve warm, split and buttered with a steaming bowl of soup.*

To freeze: *cool completely. Separate scones and pack into a large plastic bag or wrap in twos in cling film. Seal, label and freeze for 3–4 months.*

To defrost: *unwrap number required and put on a baking sheet, cook at 350°F, 180°C, Gas 4 for 15 minutes until hot.*

To microwave: *cook two at a time on full power for 1 minute.*

Sausages in blankets

Quick to make.

Uses store cupboard ingredients.

Ingredients tip Don't have any whole grain mustard then use Dijon or half the quantity of English mustard.

Serves 8   Costs ££

16 slices white bread

3 oz (75 g) soft margarine

2 tbsp coarse grain mustard

1 lb (450 g) thin sausages

1 Trim crusts off bread, spread with margarine and then spread a line of mustard diagonally across each slice of bread.

2 Separate sausages and place a sausage on each line of mustard. Bring two corners of bread up and over a sausage and secure with half a cocktail stick. Repeat with remaining sausages.

3 Spread outsides of bread with remaining margarine.

To serve now: *preheat oven to 400°F, 200°C, Gas 6. Put sausages on a baking sheet and cook for 25 minutes until sausages are browned and bread is golden.*

To freeze: *wrap sausages in twos in cling film and then put all parcels into a large plastic bag. Seal, label and freeze for 2–3 months.*

49

To defrost: *take out as many portions as required. Defrost in wrapping for 2 hours at room temperature. Cook as To serve now.*

Cheese and onion toasties

Ingredients tip Buy cheaper mild cheddar as onion and sauce adds flavour

Vegetarian tip Check label to make sure cheese is suitable for vegetarians.

Serves 8   Costs ££

10 oz (275 g) cheddar cheese

1 onion

1 egg, size 3

2 tbsp Worcestershire sauce

8 slices bread

1 Grate cheese and put into a bowl. Finely chop onion and add to cheese.

2 Beat egg, add to cheese with Worcestershire sauce and mix together.

3 Lightly toast bread on both sides then spread one side of each with cheese mixture.

To serve now: *return to grill and cook for 2–3 minutes until topping is melted and browned. Cut into triangles and serve with Mushroom and thyme soup p. 40.*

To freeze: *wrap each slice of toast in cling film. Seal, label and freeze for 2–3 months.*

To defrost: *take out as many portions as required and defrost for 2 hours at room temperature. Unwrap and grill for 3–4 minutes until piping hot in the centre.*

To microwave: *cook one slice at a time on defrost (30 per cent) for 2 minutes. Then unwrap and grill for 3–4 minutes.*

Pesto pizzas

Ingredients tip Pesto is a rich Italian basil sauce, sold in jars alongside the tubes of tomato purée. Keep in the fridge once opened.

Suitable for a vegetarian
Check the cheese label before using.

Serves 8 Costs ££

8 slices bread
little margarine for spreading
1 tbsp pesto
4 tsp tomato purée
4 tomatoes
10 oz (275 g) cheddar cheese

I Lightly toast bread on both sides then spread with margarine, pesto and tomato purée.

2 Thinly slice tomatoes and cheese and arrange on top of bread.

To serve now: cook under a hot grill for 2–3 minutes until cheese is bubbling. Cut into squares to serve.

To freeze: wrap each slice in cling film. Seal, label and freeze for 2–3 months.

To defrost: take out as many portions as required and defrost for 2 hours at room temperature. Unwrap and grill for 3–4 minutes until piping hot in the centre.

To microwave: cook one slice at a time on defrost (30 per cent) for 2 minutes. Then unwrap and grill for 3–4 minutes.

Spicy beef pockets

Ingredients tip No need to stick edges of bread with egg, just press well with fingertips.

Expert tip Covering rising bread with oiled cling film helps give a soft crust.

Serves 8   Costs ££

12 oz (350 g) minced beef or lamb

10 oz (284 g) can medium curry sauce

10 oz (280 g) pkt bread mix

little flour for dusting

1 Dry fry mince in a saucepan, stirring until browned.

2 Stir in curry sauce and water as directed on can. Cover and simmer for 20 minutes, stirring occasionally.

3 Make up bread mix according to packet directions. Knead for 5 minutes then cut into eight pieces.

4 Roll out one piece on a floured surface until the size of a tea plate. Spoon one-eighth of the mince mixture into the centre then fold dough over and press edges together to seal. Put on to an oiled baking sheet.

5 Repeat until eight pasties have been made. Cover with oiled cling film and leave to rise in a warm place.

6 Preheat oven to 425°F, 220°C, Gas 7. Remove cling film, sprinkle with flour and cook for 20 minutes until pale golden.

To serve now: serve hot with Spiced dahl soup p.41.

To freeze: *cool completely. Wrap individually in foil or cling film. Seal, label and freeze for 2–3 months.*

To defrost: *take out as many as required. Leave to defrost at room temperature for 4 hours. Unwrap, put on a baking sheet, cover tops with foil and reheat at 375°F, 190°C, Gas 5 for 20 minutes.*

Freezeable sandwiches

Freezing a few rounds of sandwiches can provide a handy snack for an elderly person. Make sandwiches in the usual way and fill with:

- *grated cheese and pickle*
- *ham and mustard*
- *liver sausage*
- *pâté*
- *smoked mackerel pâté.*

Avoid:

- *hard-boiled eggs which go rubbery on thawing*
- *salad ingredients which go very limp and watery*
- *jam which makes the bread go soggy.*

Pack rounds in cling film, seal, label and freeze for up to 2 months. Defrost in wrappings for 3 hours at room temperature.

MEAT FREE SUPPERS

Chillied marrow and mushrooms

Winter vegetable gratin

Root vegetable jalousie

Saucy spinach pasta

Double decker pasta

Tuna and sweetcorn fish cakes

Cheesy tuna and mushroom crumble

Red lentil goulash

Stuffed courgettes

Falafel

Orange, lentil and aubergine pilau

Spicy carrot dahl

Cheesy jacket potatoes

Tricolore tart

Glamorgan sausages

Chillied marrow and mush-rooms

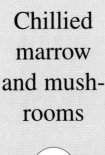

Serves 8   Costs ££

1 onion

1 small marrow about 2¼ lb (1kg)

1 lb (450 g) button mushrooms

2 tbsp oil

2 cloves garlic, crushed

½ tsp chilli powder

½ tsp ground cumin

1 tsp ground coriander

1 bay leaf

1 tsp sugar

1¾ lb (800 g) can tomatoes

¼pt (150 ml) vegetable stock

15 oz (420 g) can red kidney beans

To serve

1 lb (450 g) long grain white rice

---

1 Peel and chop onion. Halve marrow lengthways, scoop out seeds with a spoon then cut into thick slices and cut away peel. Cut into chunks. Wipe and thickly slice mushrooms.

2 Heat oil in a large saucepan, add onion and fry until golden. Add marrow and mushrooms and fry for 2 minutes.

3 Stir in garlic, spices, bay leaf and sugar and cook for 2 minutes.

4 Stir in tomatoes, stock and drained kidney beans. Season well with salt and pepper. Bring to the boil, then cover and simmer for 45 minutes.

5 Cook rice in a saucepan of boiling salted water for 8–10 minutes until tender, drain and rinse with hot water.

Cooking tip Casserole in the oven at 180°C, 350°F, Gas mark 4 for 45 minutes if preferred.

Ingredients tip This quantity of chilli powder is for hot chilli powder from an Asian supermarket.

To serve now: spoon rice on to plates and top with chilli mixture.

To freeze: cool completely. Pack portions of rice and chilli into separate bags. Seal, label and freeze for 2–3 months.

To defrost: put a portion of rice and chilli on to a plate and defrost for 4 hours at room temperature. Take chilli out of bag and reheat in a saucepan. Steam rice above in a sieve, covered with pan lid, for 5–8 minutes, stirring twice.

To microwave: remove metal tags and microwave one portion of chilli in bag on a micro-proof serving plate on full power for 5 minutes. Microwave rice in bag on full power for 2 minutes. Spoon rice and chilli on to a plate and microwave for 1 more minute.

Winter vegetable gratin

Shopping tip Look out for bargain priced vegetables at your local street market. Cheese varies in price so shop around.

Serves 8   Costs £££

12 oz (350 g) Brussels sprouts

12 oz (350 g) leeks

1 lb (450 g) broccoli

1 cauliflower

Sauce

2 oz (50 g) soft margarine

2 oz (50 g) plain flour

1½pt (900 ml) milk

8 oz (225 g) cheddar cheese

4 tsp Dijon mustard

Topping

4 oz (100 g) cheddar cheese

2 oz (50 g) breadcrumbs

little paprika

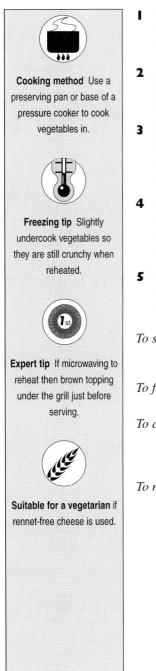

Cooking method Use a preserving pan or base of a pressure cooker to cook vegetables in.

Freezing tip Slightly undercook vegetables so they are still crunchy when reheated.

Expert tip If microwaving to reheat then brown topping under the grill just before serving.

Suitable for a vegetarian if rennet-free cheese is used.

1 Trim and halve sprouts. Trim, wash and thickly slice leeks. Cut broccoli and cauliflower into florets, stems into slices.

2 Cook vegetables in a large saucepan of boiling water for 8–10 minutes until just tender. Drain.

3 Dry pan and melt margarine. Stir in flour then gradually whisk in milk and bring to the boil, whisking until thickened and smooth.

4 Grate cheese, stir into sauce with mustard and plenty of salt and pepper. Add vegetables and toss in sauce. Divide between eight individual dishes.

5 Grate remaining cheese for topping and mix with breadcrumbs. Spoon over dishes and sprinkle with paprika.

To serve now: *cook in a preheated oven set to 425°F, 220°C, Gas 7 for 25 minutes or until topping is browned.*

To freeze: *cool completely. Cover, seal and label. Freeze for 1 month.*

To defrost: *take out as many portions as required and defrost at room temperature for 4 hours. Uncover, reheat as To serve now.*

To microwave: *cover microproof dish with pierced cling film, microwave one portion at a time on full power for 5 minutes. Leave to stand for 5 minutes then remove cling film and brown under a hot grill.*

Root vegetable jalousie

Cooking tip Don't overcook vegetables or sauce and veg will be the same texture.

Expert tip Foil dishes come in packs of 10, use an empty upturned dish to cut pastry lid.

Freezing tip Frozen puff pastry is one of the few ingredients that can be refrozen without being cooked.

Suitable for a vegetarian.

Serves 8   Costs ££

9 oz (250 g) carrot

9 oz (250 g) parsnip

9 oz (250 g) swede

1 onion

1oz (25 g) soft margarine

1 tbsp oil

2 tsp ground coriander

1 oz (25 g) plain flour

18 fl oz (500 ml) milk

2 tsp Dijon mustard

1 lb 2 oz (500 g) frozen puff pastry, defrosted

1 egg size 3, beaten

1 Peel and dice root vegetables. Cook in a saucepan of boiling salted water for 8–10 minutes until just tender. Drain.

2 Finely chop onion. Dry pan and heat margarine and oil. Fry onion until golden then stir in coriander and cook for 1 minute. Stir in flour then gradually stir in milk, bring to the boil, stirring until thickened and smooth.

3 Stir in mustard, plenty of salt and pepper and the drained vegetables. Divide mixture between eight individual foil pie dishes.

4 Cut the pastry into eight. Roll one piece out on a lightly floured surface until a little larger than top of pie dish. Cut around dish.

5 Cut extra pastry into strips and stick to edge of pie dish with a little egg. Brush top of strips with egg and press pastry lid in position. Trim edges then make cuts in the

top of the pastry. Repeat to make eight
pies. Brush pastry with egg.

To serve now: *cook in a preheated oven set to 425°F,
220°C, Gas 7 for 25–30 minutes until
pastry is well risen and golden.*

To freeze: *put pies on a baking sheet and open
freeze until solid. Cover with cling film,
seal and label. Freeze for 3–4 months.*

To defrost: *take out as many pies as required and
defrost for 4 hours at room tempera-
ture. Remove wrapping, Cook as To
serve now.*

Saucy spinach pasta

Serves 8   Costs ££

1 lb (450 g) pasta spirals

1 lb 2 oz (500 g) frozen spinach, defrosted

9 oz (250 g) cheddar cheese

2 oz (50 g) soft margarine

2 oz (50 g) plain flour

1½ pt (900 ml) milk

¼ tsp grated nutmeg

Shopping tip Buy frozen
spinach from your local
freezer centre, much
cheaper than the
supermarkets.

Freezing tip Pack pasta
into a china dish and cover
with cling film if planning to
microwave later.

1 Cook pasta in a large saucepan of boiling
water for 10–12 minutes until just tender.

2 Put spinach into a sieve and squeeze out the
water with the back of a spoon. Grate the
cheese.

3 Drain pasta into a large colander. Dry pan
and melt margarine. Stir in flour then gradually whisk in milk and bring to the boil,
whisking until thickened and smooth.

4 Reserve one quarter of the cheese and stir
remainder into sauce with the spinach, nutmeg and plenty of salt and pepper. Add the
pasta and toss in the sauce. Divide mixture

59

Serving tip Serve with grilled bacon for non vegetarians.

Suitable for a vegetarian if rennet-free cheese is used.

between eight individual dishes and sprinkle with the remaining cheese.

To serve now: *cook under a hot grill until lightly browned.*

To freeze: *cool completely. Cover, seal and label. Freeze for 1 month.*

To defrost: *take out as many portions as required and defrost for 3 hours at room temperature. Remove wrapping and cook in a preheated oven set to 425°F, 225°C, Gas 7 for 20–25 minutes until piping hot.*

To microwave: *cover microproof dish with pierced cling film and cook one portion at a time on full power for 5 minutes. Remove wrapper and brown under a hot grill.*

Expert tip If you only have dried marjoram then use a little fresh or frozen chopped parsley for colour.

Ingredients tip Add a few sliced peppers and mushrooms if available. Omit the garlic if preferred.

Double decker pasta

Serves 8   Costs ££

1 lb (450 g) pasta shells or twists

Tomato sauce

2 onions

2 tbsp oil

1 lb (450 g) courgettes

2 cloves garlic, crushed

1¾ lb (800 g) can tomatoes

1 tbsp tomato purée

¼ pt (150 ml) vegetable stock

2 tbsp fresh chopped marjoram or 1 tsp dried

1 tsp sugar

Marjoram sauce

2 oz (50 g) soft margarine

2 oz (50 g) plain flour

1¼ pt (750 ml) milk

2 tbsp fresh chopped marjoram or 1 tsp dried

2 tbsp grated parmesan

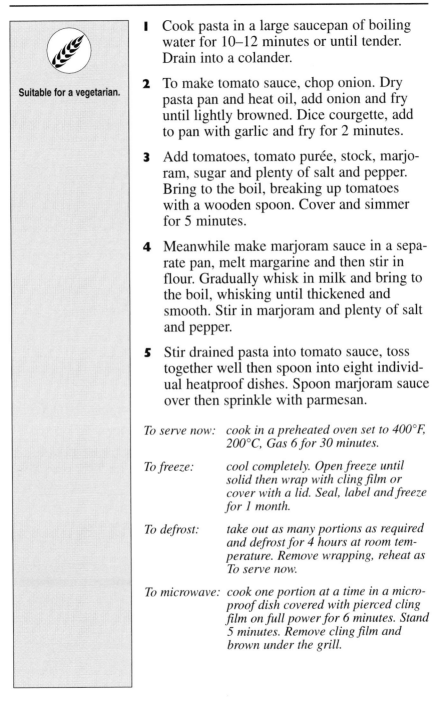

Suitable for a vegetarian.

I Cook pasta in a large saucepan of boiling water for 10–12 minutes or until tender. Drain into a colander.

2 To make tomato sauce, chop onion. Dry pasta pan and heat oil, add onion and fry until lightly browned. Dice courgette, add to pan with garlic and fry for 2 minutes.

3 Add tomatoes, tomato purée, stock, marjoram, sugar and plenty of salt and pepper. Bring to the boil, breaking up tomatoes with a wooden spoon. Cover and simmer for 5 minutes.

4 Meanwhile make marjoram sauce in a separate pan, melt margarine and then stir in flour. Gradually whisk in milk and bring to the boil, whisking until thickened and smooth. Stir in marjoram and plenty of salt and pepper.

5 Stir drained pasta into tomato sauce, toss together well then spoon into eight individual heatproof dishes. Spoon marjoram sauce over then sprinkle with parmesan.

To serve now: *cook in a preheated oven set to 400°F, 200°C, Gas 6 for 30 minutes.*

To freeze: *cool completely. Open freeze until solid then wrap with cling film or cover with a lid. Seal, label and freeze for 1 month.*

To defrost: *take out as many portions as required and defrost for 4 hours at room temperature. Remove wrapping, reheat as To serve now.*

To microwave: *cook one portion at a time in a micro-proof dish covered with pierced cling film on full power for 6 minutes. Stand 5 minutes. Remove cling film and brown under the grill.*

Tuna and sweetcorn fish cakes

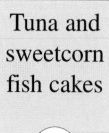

Ingredients tip If using tuna in oil then use a little oil from the can for frying the leek.

Expert tip Don't have heat too high when frying frozen fish cakes or the outside will be done before the inside is hot.

Serving tip Serve with salad.

Serves 8   Costs ££

2¼ lb (1kg) potatoes

8oz (225 g) leek

2oz (50 g) soft margarine

2 × 7 oz (200 g) cans tuna chunks

6 oz (150 g) frozen sweetcorn

1 lemon, grated rind and juice

2 eggs, size 3

2 tbsp milk

6 oz (150 g) breadcrumbs

little oil for frying

---

1 Peel and halve potatoes. Cook in a large saucepan of boiling water until tender.

2 Trim, rinse and finely chop leek. Melt margarine in a frying pan, add leek and cook for 2–3 minutes until softened.

3 Add drained tuna and break into pieces, then add sweetcorn, lemon rind and juice and plenty of salt and pepper.

4 Drain and mash potato. Stir tuna mixture into potato and mix together well. Leave to cool.

5 Divide the mixture into 16 on a floured board then pat into rounds with floured hands.

6 Beat eggs and milk together on a plate. Put breadcrumbs on a second plate. Coat fish cakes in egg then breadcrumbs and put on a baking sheet.

To serve now: *heat a little oil in a large frying pan and fry fish cakes in batches until browned on both sides and hot through.*

To freeze: *open-freeze until solid. Remove from baking sheet and pack in a plastic box, interleaving layers with foil. Seal, label and freeze for 3–4 months.*

To defrost: *heat a little oil in a frying pan, add as many frozen fish cakes as required, cover and fry over a medium heat for 10–12 minutes, turning several times until browned and hot through.*

Cheesy tuna and mushroom crumble

Ingredients tip Use fresh parsley or chives from the garden.

Expert tip Tuna mixture can be served without crumble, as a pasta sauce or with mashed potatoes and peas.

Serves 8   **Costs ££**

Sauce

2 oz (50 g) soft margarine

2 oz (50 g) plain flour

1½pt (900 ml) milk

8 oz (225 g) button mushrooms

4 oz (100 g) frozen sweetcorn

5 tbsp fresh chopped parsley

2 × 7 oz (200 g) cans tuna chunks

Crumble

6 oz (150 g) plain flour

3 oz (75 g) soft margarine

3 oz (75 g) cheddar cheese

1 To make sauce, melt margarine in a saucepan then stir in flour. Gradually whisk in milk and bring to the boil, whisking until thickened and smooth.

2 Wipe and slice mushrooms, add to sauce and cook for 2 minutes.

3 Stir in sweetcorn, parsley, drained tuna and plenty of salt and pepper. Divide mixture between eight individual dishes.

4 To make crumble, put flour and a little salt

and pepper into a bowl. Add margarine, cut into pieces and rub in with fingertips until mixture resembles fine breadcrumbs.

5 Grate cheese and stir into crumble. Divide between dishes.

To serve now: *cook in a preheated oven set to 400°F, 200°C, Gas 6 for 35 minutes or until crumble has browned.*

To freeze: *cool completely. Overwrap in cling film, seal and label. Freeze for 1 month.*

To defrost: *take out as many portions as required and defrost for 3 hours at room temperature. Remove wrapper and cook as To serve now.*

Red lentil goulash

Serving tip Serve with frozen garlic bread or brown rice.

Expert tip You may need to add a little extra stock towards the end of cooking.

Suitable for a vegetarian.

Serves 8   Costs ££

2 onions

1½ lb (675 g) carrots

1 lb 2 oz (500 g) potatoes

6 sticks celery

2 tbsp oil

3 cloves garlic, crushed

2 tbsp paprika

¼–½ tsp chilli powder

1 tsp caraway seeds

2 pt (1.1 litre) vegetable stock

2 tbsp tomato purée

2 tbsp brown sugar

8 oz (225 g) red lentils

4 oz (100 g) green cabbage

I Peel and chop onions. Peel and dice carrots. Peel and cut potatoes into large chunks. Wash and thickly slice celery.

2 Heat oil in a large frying pan, add onion and fry until golden. Add carrots, potatoes, celery and garlic and fry for 2 minutes.

3 Stir in paprika, chilli and caraway seeds and fry for 1 minute.

4 Pour on stock then stir in tomato purée, sugar and plenty of salt and pepper. Stir in lentils, bring to the boil then cover and simmer for 30 minutes until lentils are tender.

5 Finely shred cabbage, add to pan, return lid and cook for 5 minutes.

To serve now: *spoon on to plates. Top with spoonfuls of natural yogurt if liked.*

To freeze: *cool completely. Pack into plastic bags, seal and label. Freeze for 2–3 months.*

To defrost: *take out as many portions as required and defrost for 4 hours at room temperature. Remove bag and tie and reheat in a saucepan until piping hot.*

To microwave: *remove tag from bag, microwave one portion at a time in a microproof serving dish on full power for 3 minutes. Remove bag, stir and loosely cover with bag. Cook for 3 minutes more until piping hot.*

Stuffed courgettes

Shopping tip Only make this recipe when courgettes are low in price.

Serves 8   Costs ££

8 small courgettes about 2 lb (900 g)

8 oz (225 g) button mushrooms

1 onion

2 tbsp oil

3 cloves garlic, crushed

1 tbsp tomato purée

Sauce

Freezing tip Sauce may seem thick but water from courgettes will help counteract this. For best results defrost and reheat in the oven.

Serving tip Serve with a green salad and new potatoes or crusty bread.

Suitable for a vegetarian.

2 oz (50 g) soft margarine

2 oz (50 g) plain flour

1pt (600 ml) milk

¼ tsp grated nutmeg

2 tbsp grated parmesan

I Wash and halve courgettes lengthways. Scoop out centres with a teaspoon leaving a thick shell. Roughly chop scooped out courgette and set aside.

2 Cook courgette shells in a large saucepan of boiling water for 4 minutes until softened. Drain into a colander, rinse with cold water and drain again.

3 Wipe and chop mushrooms. Chop onion. Heat oil in a frying pan and fry mushrooms and onion until softened.

4 Add chopped courgette and garlic and fry for 2 minutes. Stir tomato purée and plenty of salt and pepper into mushroom mixture.

5 Arrange 2 courgette shells, cut side uppermost in base of eight individual heatproof dishes. Then divide mushroom mixture between courgettes.

6 To make the sauce, melt the margarine in dried courgette pan. Stir in flour then gradually add milk, and bring to the boil, stirring until thickened and smooth.

7 Stir nutmeg and plenty of salt and pepper into sauce then spoon over courgettes. Sprinkle with parmesan.

To serve now: *cook in a preheated oven set to 400°F, 200°C, Gas 6 for 30 minutes until browned.*

To freeze: *cool completely. Open-freeze until*

solid then wrap in cling film or cover with a lid. Seal, label and freeze for 4–6 months.

To defrost: take out as many portions as required and defrost for 4 hours at room temperature. Uncover and cook as To serve now.

To microwave: cook one portion at a time in a micro-proof serving dish covered with pierced cling film on full power for 4 minutes. Remove cling film and brown under a hot grill.

Falfel

Serves 8   Costs £

12 oz (350 g) dried chick peas, soaked overnight in cold water

2 onions

2 oz (50 g) parsley

2 cloves garlic, crushed

2 tsp ground cumin

1 tbsp ground coriander

oil for frying

Ingredients tip If you don't have any chick peas or not enough, then use mixed dried pulses.

Cooking method If you don't have a food processor or mincer, then mash peas, finely chop onion and parsley, then mix together with garlic and spices.

Healthy tip Very high in fibre.

1 Drain chick peas, put into a saucepan, cover with cold water and bring to the boil. Boil rapidly for 10 minutes then reduce the heat and simmer for 1 hour or until tender.

2 Drain peas and put into a food processor or mincer. Roughly chop onion and parsley. Finely chop chick peas, onion and parsley in a food processor or mince twice. Mix with garlic, spices and plenty of salt and pepper.

4 Shape into small balls about the size of a walnut and put on a large baking sheet.

To serve now: chill for 30 minutes then shallow fry in batches until crisp and brown on the

67

Suitable for a vegetarian.

Serving tip Serve with a tomato salad and diced cucumber tossed in a little natural yogurt flavoured with mint.

outside. Drain well on kitchen paper and serve hot.

To freeze: *open-freeze until solid then pack into a plastic box, interleaving layers with foil. Seal, label and freeze for 4–6 months.*

To defrost: *shallow fry falafel from frozen over a moderate to low heat for 5 minutes, turning frequently until browned and hot through. Drain on kitchen paper before serving.*

Orange, lentil and aubergine pilau

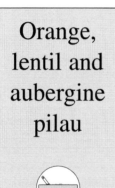

Ingredients tip Stir in a little frozen spinach just before reheating.

Healthy tip High in fibre.

Serves 8   Costs ££

2 onions

2 small aubergines or 1½lb (675 g)

4 tbsp oil

12 oz (350 g) brown rice

2 cloves garlic, crushed

8 oz (225 g) green lentils

1pt (600 ml) orange juice from a carton of long life orange juice

2 pt (1.1 litre) vegetable stock

2 tbsp tomato purée

2 tsp ground cinnamon

2 oz (50 g) currants

8 oz (225 g) frozen peas

I   Chop onion and cut aubergine into large dice discarding stalk. Heat oil in a large saucepan or wok and fry onion and aubergine until browned.

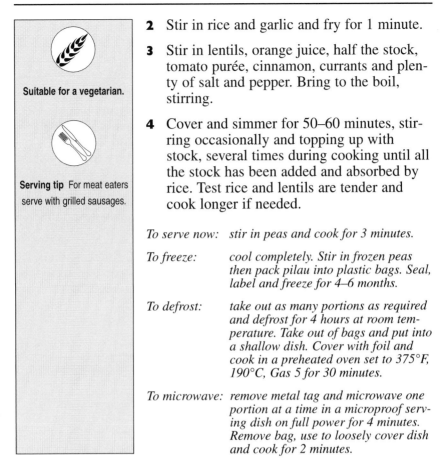

2 Stir in rice and garlic and fry for 1 minute.

3 Stir in lentils, orange juice, half the stock, tomato purée, cinnamon, currants and plenty of salt and pepper. Bring to the boil, stirring.

4 Cover and simmer for 50–60 minutes, stirring occasionally and topping up with stock, several times during cooking until all the stock has been added and absorbed by rice. Test rice and lentils are tender and cook longer if needed.

To serve now: *stir in peas and cook for 3 minutes.*

To freeze: *cool completely. Stir in frozen peas then pack pilau into plastic bags. Seal, label and freeze for 4–6 months.*

To defrost: *take out as many portions as required and defrost for 4 hours at room temperature. Take out of bags and put into a shallow dish. Cover with foil and cook in a preheated oven set to 375°F, 190°C, Gas 5 for 30 minutes.*

To microwave: *remove metal tag and microwave one portion at a time in a microproof serving dish on full power for 4 minutes. Remove bag, use to loosely cover dish and cook for 2 minutes.*

Spicy carrot dahl

Serves 8   **Costs ££**

2 onions

2 lb (900 g) carrots

2 tbsp oil

½ tsp chilli powder

2 tsp turmeric

2 tsp ground cumin

2 tsp ground ginger

4 tsp ground coriander

69

12 oz (350 g) red lentils

2½ pt (1.5 litre) vegetable stock

1 cauliflower

I Peel and chop onions. Peel and dice carrots. Heat oil in a large saucepan or preserving pan. Add onion and fry until lightly browned. Add carrots and fry for 2 minutes.

2 Stir in spices and cook for 1 minute. Add lentils, stock and plenty of salt and pepper. Bring to the boil, stirring then cover and simmer for 40 minutes.

3 Cut cauliflower into small florets and any leaves into pieces. Add to pan and cook for 10 minutes, stirring occasionally.

To serve now: *serve dahl on a bed of rice.*

To freeze: *cool completely then spoon portions of dahl into small plastic bags. Seal, label and freeze for 2–3 months.*

To defrost: *take out as many portions as required and defrost for 4 hours at room temperature. Take dahl out of bag and reheat in a saucepan, stirring until piping hot.*

To microwave: *remove metal tag and put one portion in a microproof serving dish. Cook on full power for 3 minutes. Remove bag, stir and loosely cover with bag, cook for 3 more minutes.*

larger more economical bags from Indian grocers. Beware – chilli powder is usually hotter than supermarket brands.

Ingredients tip For a hot curry add 1 tsp chilli powder.

Expert tip This is quite a runny curry, simmer without a lid for 5 minutes more before adding cauliflower if you prefer thicker sauces.

Freezing tip Freeze portion sized bags of cooked rice if liked. See p.56 on how to reheat.

Suitable for a vegetarian.

Cheesy jacket potatoes

Ingredients tip Use fresh herbs from the garden, don't buy specially.

Suitable for a vegetarian.

Serving tip Serve with grilled bacon for meat eaters.

Serves 8   Costs £££

8 baking potatoes, about 5½ lb (2.5 kg)

2 oz (50 g) soft margarine

4 eggs, size 3

6 oz (150 g) cheddar cheese

1 tbsp Dijon mustard

2 tbsp fresh chopped chives, tarragon or parsley, optional

3 tomatoes

---

1 Preheat oven to 375°F, 190°C, Gas 5. Scrub and prick potatoes and bake straight on oven shelf for 1¼–2 hours until tender.

2 Cut potatoes in half and scoop out centres to leave a thick shell. Mash centres with margarine and plenty of salt and pepper.

3 Beat eggs together. Grate cheese. Stir eggs and cheese into mashed potato with mustard and herbs.

4 Spoon back into potato shells. Slice tomatoes and add a slice to each potato.

To serve now: *put potatoes on a baking sheet and cook in a preset oven to 400°F, 200°C, Gas 6 for 25–30 minutes until browned. Serve hot.*

To freeze: *wrap in cling film and freeze on a tray until solid. Pack into a plastic box, seal, label and freeze for 4–6 months.*

To defrost: *take out as many portions as required and defrost for 4 hours at room temperature. Remove cling film and cook as To serve now.*

To microwave: *put 2 halves on a microproof plate, loosen cling film and cook on full power for 4 minutes. Remove cling film and grill until browned.*

71

Tricolore Tart

Shopping tip Cheddar cheese varies enormously in price, shop around for best buys and choose a medium strength cheese.

Expert tip Best not to reheat portions of tart in the microwave, pastry tends to go soggy.

Suitable for a vegetarian but use rennet-free cheese.

Serves 8   Costs ££

Pastry

8 oz (225 g) plain flour

2 oz (50 g) block margarine

2 oz (50 g) white vegetable fat

Filling

1 tbsp Dijon mustard

5 oz (125 g) cheddar cheese

1 small leek

1 red pepper

4 oz (100 g) button mushrooms

4 eggs, size 3

¾ pt (450 ml) milk

1 Put flour and a pinch of salt into a bowl. Add fats cut into pieces and rub in with fingertips until fine breadcrumbs.

2 Add 3 tbsp water and mix to a smooth dough. Knead lightly then roll out thinly on a floured surface.

3 Use to line an 11 inch (28 cm) loose bottomed flan tin. Chill for 15 minutes.

4 Preheat oven to 375°F, 190°C, Gas 5. Spread mustard over base of tart. Put tin on a baking sheet. Grate cheese and sprinkle two thirds over the mustard.

5 Trim and wash leek then thinly slice. Chop red pepper, discarding core and seeds. Cook both in a saucepan of boiling water for 1 minute. Drain and add to tart with sliced mushrooms and remaining cheese.

6 Beat eggs, milk and plenty of salt and pepper together. Pour over tart and cook for 50 minutes until golden and filling is set.

To serve now: cut into wedges and serve warm with salad and new potatoes.

To freeze: cool completely. Cut into wedges and wrap in foil. Seal, label and freeze for 3–4 months.

To defrost: take out as many portions as required for 4 hours at room temperature. Open out foil and reheat in a preset 400°F, 200°C, Gas 6 oven for 25 minutes.

Glamorgan sausages

Shopping tip Can also use Cheshire or Cheddar cheese.

Ingredients tip Use two onions instead of leeks if preferred.

Serving tip Sausages are very rich so serve with grilled tomatoes and peas.

Serves 8   Costs ££

9 oz (250 g) Caerphilly cheese

12 oz (350 g) leek

1 lb (450 g) breadcrumbs

4 eggs, size 3, separated

3 tsp Dijon mustard

2 tbsp fresh thyme leaves or 1 tsp dried

oil for shallow frying

1 Grate cheese into a bowl. Trim, rinse and finely chop leeks. Add to cheese with 12 oz (350 g) breadcrumbs and mix together.

2 Put egg whites on to a large plate or into a shallow dish. Put yolks into a small bowl and stir in mustard, thyme and plenty of salt and pepper.

3 Add yolks to cheese mixture and mix together well. Divide into 16 mounds on a chopping board then shape each mound into a sausage about 4 inch (10 cm) long.

4 Dip each sausage into egg white then roll in remaining breadcrumbs and put on to a baking sheet. Chill until required.

73

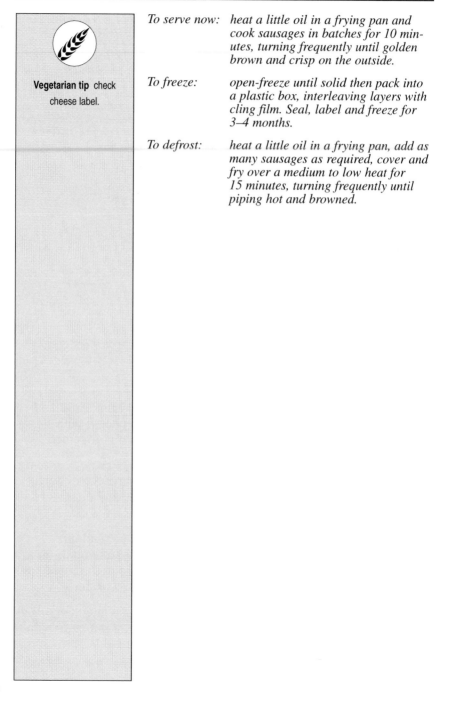

Vegetarian tip check cheese label.

To serve now: *heat a little oil in a frying pan and cook sausages in batches for 10 minutes, turning frequently until golden brown and crisp on the outside.*

To freeze: *open-freeze until solid then pack into a plastic box, interleaving layers with cling film. Seal, label and freeze for 3–4 months.*

To defrost: *heat a little oil in a frying pan, add as many sausages as required, cover and fry over a medium to low heat for 15 minutes, turning frequently until piping hot and browned.*

COMPLETE MEALS

Vegetable shepherd's pie

Carpaccio

Tamal beef and polenta pie

Spinach sausages with garlicky tomato sauce

Faggots

Corned beef and tattie pie

Shepherd's pie

Mediterranean lamb with rosemary and brown rice

Hot Sussex smokies

Jumbalaya

Vegetable shepherd's pie

Serves 8   **Costs ££**

9 oz (250 g) bag mixed dried pulses, soaked overnight in cold water

1 onion

12 oz (350 g) carrots

3 sticks celery

1 tbsp oil

1¾ lb (800 g) can tomatoes

½ pt (300 ml) vegetable stock

2 tsp sugar

small bunch fresh herbs or 1 tsp dried

Topping

3 lb (1.4 kg) potatoes

2 oz (50 g) soft margarine

2 eggs, size 3, beaten

8 oz (225 g) cheddar cheese

little paprika

1 Drain beans, put into a saucepan, cover with fresh cold water and bring to the boil. Boil rapidly for 10 minutes then reduce heat slightly and cook for 1 hour or until beans are tender. Drain.

2 Peel and chop onion. Peel and dice carrot. Wash and slice celery.

3 Heat oil in a large saucepan, fry onion until lightly browned. Add carrots and celery and fry for 2 minutes.

4 Stir in tomatoes, stock, sugar, herbs and plenty of seasoning. Bring to the boil then cover and simmer for 20 minutes or until sauce is thick and vegetables are tender.

5 Meanwhile, peel potatoes, cut in half and cook in boiling water until tender. Drain

and mash with margarine and plenty of salt and pepper.

6 Beat eggs together, grate cheese and reserve one third. Stir remaining cheese and eggs into potato.

7 Divide bean mixture between eight individual dishes and top with potato. Sprinkle with remaining cheese and paprika.

To serve now: cook in a preheated oven set to 400°F, 200°C, Gas 6 for 35 minutes until browned.

To freeze: cool completely. Cover with foil or cling film, seal and label. Freeze up to 4–6 months.

To defrost: take out as many portions as required and defrost at room temperature for 5 hours. Uncover, cook as To serve now.

To microwave: cook one portion at a time in a micro-proof dish covered with pierced cling film on defrost (30 per cent) for 12 minutes then full power for 2½ minutes.

Carpaccio

Shopping tip Look out for mince on special offer, buy two packs when cheap and freeze until required.

Expert tip Transfer to a plate to microwave if frozen

Serves 8   Costs £££

2 onions

2 lb (900 g) frozen minced beef or lamb

3 cloves garlic, crushed

2 tsp mixed dried herbs

½ tsp ground cinnamon

1¾ lb (800 g) can tomatoes

2 tbsp tomato purée

12 oz (350 g) courgettes

12 oz (350 g) pasta twists

2 oz (50 g) soft margarine

2 oz (50 g) plain flour

1¼ pt (750 ml) milk

77

4 oz (100 g) cheddar cheese

little paprika

in a foil dish. Run base of dish under hot tap, for easy removal.

Cooking method A good party dish if frozen in one large dish. Defrost overnight at room temperature. Cook at 400°F, 200°C, Gas 6 for 1 hour.

1 Chop onions and add to a large saucepan with mince. Dry fry over a gentle heat, stirring occasionally until evenly browned.

2 Add garlic, herbs, cinnamon, tomatoes, tomato purée and ½ pt (300 ml) water. Season well and bring to the boil. Cover and simmer for 20 minutes, stirring occasionally.

3 Dice courgettes and add to mince, cook for 5 minutes.

4 Meanwhile half fill a second large pan with water, bring to boil, add pasta and cook for 10 minutes. Drain, rinse with water and drain again.

5 Dry pasta pan and melt margarine. Stir in flour then gradually stir in milk and bring to the boil, stirring until thickened and smooth.

6 Grate cheese and stir two thirds into sauce with plenty of salt and pepper and drained pasta.

7 Spoon mince into eight individual foil or china dishes then spoon pasta mixture on top. Sprinkle with cheese and paprika.

To serve now: cook at 400°F, 200°C, Gas 6 for 35 minutes until browned. Serve with a salad.

To freeeze: cool completely. Cover with foil lid or cling film. Seal, label and freeze up to 1 month.

To defrost: leave for 5 hours at room temperature. Remove lid or wrapping and cook as To serve now.

To microwave: cook one portion at a time in a micro-proof dish covered with pierced cling film on defrost (30 per cent) for 20 minutes. Break block up slightly so centre heats up, then cook on full power for 3 minutes.

Tamal beef and polenta pie

Ingredients tip Chilli powder varies in strength, this quantity is for hot chilli powder from an Asian supermarket. Can also use minced pork.

Expert tip Don't cook polenta over too high a heat or it may burn as it thickens.

Freezing tip Transfer to a plate to microwave if frozen in a foil dish.

Serves 8   Costs £££

2 onions

2 lb (900 g) minced beef

½ tsp hot chilli powder

1 tsp ground cumin

2 cloves garlic, crushed

1¾ lb (800 g) can tomatoes

½ pt (300 ml) beef stock

2 tsp sugar

2 tbsp tomato purée

13 oz (375 g) pack polenta (pre-cooked maize meal)

little oil for greasing

2 oz (50 g) cheddar cheese

1 Chop onions, put into a large saucepan with the mince and dry fry, stirring until mince is evenly browned.

2 Stir in chilli powder, cumin and garlic and fry for 2 minutes.

3 Add tomatoes, stock, sugar, tomato purée and plenty of seasoning. Bring to the boil, breaking up mince and tomatoes with a spoon.

4 Cover and simmer for 45 minutes, stirring occasionally.

5 Meanwhile bring a pan of water to the boil,

79

see polenta pack for quantities. Line a small roasting tin with foil and brush with oil.

6 Add polenta to water with 2 tsp salt and cook, stirring constantly for 5–10 minutes until very thick.

7 Spoon polenta into roasting tin, level with a wooden spoon or wetted hands. Leave to cool.

8 Spoon mince into eight individual oven-proof or foil dishes. Lift foil and polenta out of roasting tin. Cut into triangles, lift off foil and arrange slightly overlapping over top of mince.

9 Grate cheese and sprinkle over polenta.

To serve now: *cook at 400°F, 200°C, Gas 6 for 45 minutes until piping hot.*

To freeze: *leave to cool completely. Wrap with cling film or foil. Seal, label and freeze up to 2–3 months.*

To defrost: *take out as many portions as required. Defrost for 5 hours at room tempera-ture. Remove wrapping and cook as To serve now.*

To microwave: *cook one portion at a time in a micro-proof dish, covered with pierced cling film on defrost (30 per cent) for 15 minutes. Then full power for 3 min-utes. Remove cling film and brown under the grill.*

Spinach sausages with garlicky tomato sauce

Serves 8   Costs ££

Sausages

8 oz (225 g) frozen leaf spinach, defrosted

2 onions

2 lb (900 g) pork sausagemeat

4 oz (100 g) white breadcrumbs

½ tsp ground cinnamon

Sauce

2 onions

2 tbsp oil

2 cloves garlic, crushed

2 tsp sugar

1¾ lb (800 g) can tomatoes

To serve

1 lb (450 g) long grain white rice

Expert tip Make sure baking sheet will fit in fridge before adding sausages.

Ingredients tip If you don't have any cinnamon then use nutmeg. Use fresh peeled tomatoes if you grow your own.

Cooking tip Cut one of the cooked sausages in half to check it is cooked right through.

1 Put spinach into a sieve and press out water with the back of a spoon.

2 Finely chop onions and put into a bowl with the spinach, sausagemeat, breadcrumbs, cinnamon and plenty of salt and pepper. Mix together with a spoon or hands.

3 Shape into 24 sausages with wet hands and put on a baking sheet lined with foil. Chill for 30 minutes.

4 To make sauce, finely chop onions and fry in oil for 5 minutes until soft. Add garlic, sugar, tomatoes and plenty of salt and pepper. Bring to boil, break up tomatoes with a spoon then simmer for 10 minutes.

5 Cook sausages under a hot grill for 15 minutes, turning three times until evenly browned and cooked through.

6 Cook rice in a saucepan of boiling salted water for 10 minutes. Drain, rinse with hot water and drain again.

7 Spoon rice into base of eight individual foil or china dishes. Arrange sausages on top and spoon sauce over.

To serve now: serve immediately.

To freeze: cool completely. Cover with foil lid or cling film. Seal, label and freeze for 2–3 months.

To defrost: leave for 4 hours at room temperature. Cover with foil and cook in preset oven 400°F, 200°C, Gas 6 for 35 minutes until piping hot.

To microwave: unwrap and transfer one portion to a microproof plate. Cover with pierced cling film and cook on defrost (30 per cent) for 15 minutes, break up block so centre reheats thoroughly, then full power for 3 minutes.

Faggots

Expert tip Traditionally wrapped in caul fat, nowadays difficult to buy, add suet to mixture instead.

Serves 8   Costs £££

1¾ lb (800 g) lambs' liver, defrosted if frozen

3 onions

4 rashers streaky bacon

10 oz (275 g) bread

6 oz (150 g) suet

2 tbsp fresh chopped sage or 1½ tsp dried

2 pt (1.1 litre) beef stock

To serve

2½ lb (1.1 kg) potatoes

8 oz (225 g) leeks

1 oz (25 g) soft margarine

2 tbsp milk

2 tbsp cornflour

1 tsp wholegrain mustard

2 tbsp Worcestershire sauce

12 oz (350 g) frozen peas

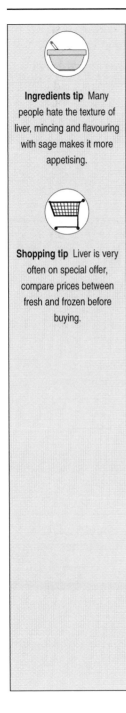

Ingredients tip Many people hate the texture of liver, mincing and flavouring with sage makes it more appetising.

Shopping tip Liver is very often on special offer, compare prices between fresh and frozen before buying.

I Rinse liver with cold water and drain well. Roughly chop liver and onions and then process until finely chopped or mince. Put into a bowl.

2 Cut rind away from bacon and roughly chop, cut bread into cubes. Process or mince.

3 Stir bacon and bread into liver mixture with suet, sage and plenty of salt and pepper. Mix together and leave to stand for 15 minutes.

4 Preheat oven to 400°F, 200°C, Gas 6. Brush a large roasting tin with a little oil. Put dessert spoonfuls of liver mixture into tin then pour over half the hot stock. Cook uncovered for 20 minutes.

5 Meanwhile cut potatoes into chunky pieces and cook in boiling water for 15 minutes. Thinly slice leeks and add to potato pan for last 3 minutes.

6 Drain and mash potatoes and leeks with margarine, milk and salt and pepper.

7 Mix cornflour with a little water in a saucepan until a smooth paste. Stir in remaining stock, mustard, Worcestershire sauce, salt and pepper and stock from roasting tin. Bring to boil, stirring until thickened and smooth.

8 Divide potato and leek between eight individual foil or china dishes. Add faggots and gravy.

To serve now: cook peas and serve with mashed potatoes, faggots and gravy.

To freeze: cool completely. Add still frozen peas, cover with foil lid or foil. Seal, label and freeze for 2–3 months.

To defrost: leave at room temperature for 5 hours. Reheat at 400°F, 200°C, Gas 6, loosely covered with foil for 40 minutes.

To microwave: unwrap and transfer one portion to a microproof plate. Cover with pierced cling film and cook on defrost (30 per cent) for 15 minutes, break up block then cook on full power for 3 minutes.

Corned beef and tattie pie

Expert tip Halve recipe if preferred.

Ingredients tip Add 2oz (50g) chopped gherkins or dill cucumbers to corned beef if liked.

Serves 8   Costs ££

1½ lb (675 g) potatoes

3 onions

2 oz (50 g) soft margarine

4 tbsp tomato ketchup

2 × 12 oz (340 g) cans corned beef

Pastry

1¼ lb (550 g) plain flour

5 oz (125 g) block margarine

5 oz (125 g) white vegetable fat

1 egg, beaten to glaze

1   Peel and cut potatoes into chunky pieces. Cook in a saucepan of boiling salted water until tender.

2   Meanwhile finely chop onions. Heat margarine in a large frying pan, add onions and fry until golden.

3   Drain and mash potatoes and stir into onion mixture with ketchup and plenty of salt and pepper. Leave to cool.

4 Chop corned beef and stir into cooled potato mixture.

5 To make pastry, put flour and a pinch of salt into a bowl, add fats cut into pieces and rub in with fingertips or an electric mixer until mixture resembles fine breadcrumbs.

6 Add 5–6 tbsp water and mix to a smooth dough. Knead lightly and cut into eight pieces.

7 Roll each piece out thinly on a floured surface and use to line eight individual foil pie dishes. Trim off excess pastry and knead together.

8 Divide corned beef mixture between pies. Brush edges of pastry with egg then. Reroll pastry trimmings and cut thin strips. Arrange strips over top of pies to form a lattice then trim edges and brush strips with egg.

To serve now: *cook at 400°F, 200°C, Gas 6 for 30–35 minutes. Serve with baked beans and peas.*

To freeze: *open-freeze pies until solid then over-wrap with cling film. Seal, label and freeze for 3–4 months.*

To defrost: *leave at room temperature for 4 hours. Remove cling film and cook and serve as To serve now.*

Shepherds pie

Ingredients tip Can also use minced lamb.

Cooking tip If there seems a lot of gravy with mince then cook uncovered for 5 minutes.

Freezing tip Portions are generous for individual foil dishes so cover with cling film.

Healthy tip Baked beans add fibre.

Serves 8   Costs £££

2 onions

2 lb (900 g) minced beef

1 lb 2 oz (500 g) carrots

2 tbsp plain flour

2 × 15 oz (420 g) cans baked beans

1 pt (600 ml) beef stock

1 tbsp tomato purée

1 tbsp Dijon mustard

2 tbsp Worcestershire sauce

Topping

1½ lb (675 g) parsnips

3½ lb (1.6k g) potatoes

3½ oz (85 g) sage and onion stuffing mix

2 oz (50 g) soft margarine

5–6 tbsp milk

1 Chop onion and dry fry in a large saucepan or wok with the mince, stirring until mince is evenly browned.

2 Dice carrots, add to pan and fry for 2 minutes. Stir in flour then add baked beans, stock, tomato purée, mustard, Worcestershire sauce and plenty of salt and pepper.

3 Bring to the boil stirring, then cover and simmer for 30 minutes, stirring occasionally.

4 Meanwhile make the topping. Peel and cut parsnips and potatoes into chunks and cook in a large saucepan until tender.

5 Drain parsnips and potatoes, reserving some of the boiling water. Measure boiling vegetable water and use to soak stuffing mix as pack directs.

6 Mash parsnips and potatoes with margarine, milk and salt and pepper. Beat in stuffing mix.

7 Spoon mince mixture into the base of eight individual heatproof dishes. Top with potato mixture.

To serve now: *cook at 400°F, 200°C, Gas 6 for 35 minutes until potato is browned.*

To freeze: *cool completely, wrap in cling film or cover with a lid. Seal, label and freeze for 4–6 months.*

To defrost: *take out as many portions as required and defrost for 5 hours at room temperature. Remove wrapper and cook as To serve now.*

To microwave: *cook one portion at a time in a microproof dish, covered with pierced cling film on defrost (30 per cent) for 15 minutes then full power for 4 minutes.*

Mediterranean lamb with rosemary and brown rice

Serves 8   Costs £££

2 tbsp oil

3½ lb (1.6 kg) neck of lamb, defrosted if frozen

2 onions

3 cloves garlic, crushed

2 tbsp plain flour

3 pt (1.7 litre) chicken stock

4 tbsp lemon juice

4 tbsp tomato purée

small bunch fresh rosemary or 1½ tsp dried

13¾ oz (390 g) can red pimientoes

14 oz (400 g) brown rice

Shopping tip There are usually three red peppers in each can of red pimientoes; check prices – can be cheaper than buying fresh.

Ingredients tip Brown rice adds a lovely nutty taste.

Expert tip You will need a very big dish or roasting tin to cook this in – a turkey roasting tin is ideal, tightly covered with foil.

1 Preheat oven to 350°F, 180°C, Gas 4. Heat oil in a large saucepan or wok, add lamb and fry in batches until browned on both sides. Drain and reserve on a baking sheet.

2 Peel and chop onion and fry in pan juices with garlic, until lightly browned.

3 Stir in flour, then mix in stock, lemon juice, tomato purée, rosemary and plenty of salt and pepper. Drain and roughly chop pimientoes. Add to pan with rice, bring to the boil, stirring.

4 Pour into a large casserole dish or deep roasting tin. Place lamb on top then cover and cook in the oven for 1¾ hours.

To serve now: *spoon on to plates.*

To freeze: *cool completely. Take meat off the bone. Spoon portions of rice into small plastic bags, divide lamb between bags, seal and label. Freeze for 4–6 months.*

To defrost: *take out as many portions as required and defrost for 5 hours at room temperature. Reheat in ovenproof dish, covered with foil at 400°F, 200°C, Gas 6 for 35 minutes.*

To microwave: *remove metal tag from bag and microwave per portion on defrost (30 per cent) for 10 minutes. Transfer to a microproof plate, loosely cover with bag and cook on full power for 3 minutes.*

Hot Sussex smokies

Ingredients tip Smoked haddock is much more expensive than its unsmoked counterpart. Layering with potato helps to extend the fish but keep all the taste.

Shopping tip Shop around the freezer centres and supermarkets for the best priced fish. Use smoked cod or whiting if available.

Serves 8   Costs £££

1¼ lb (600 g) bag frozen smoked haddock fillets

2 bay leaves

3 lb (1.4 kg) potatoes

12 oz (350 g) leeks

Sauce

¾ pt (450 ml) milk

6 oz (150 g) cheddar cheese

3 oz (75 g) soft margarine

3 oz (75 g) plain flour

¼ tsp grated nutmeg

I Put fish in a large saucepan or frying pan with bay leaves, little ground pepper and ¾ pt (450 ml) water. Cover and simmer for 10 minutes until fish is cooked and flakes when pressed with a knife.

2 Transfer fish to a large plate, peel away skin and break fish into large flakes, discarding any bones. Reserve fish liquor.

3 Peel and thinly slice potatoes, add to a large saucepan of boiling water and cook for 4 minutes until just tender. Trim, wash and thinly slice leeks. Add to potatoes for last minute of cooking.

4 Drain potatoes and leeks in a colander, rinse with cold water and drain.

5 Pour fish liquor into a measuring jug and make up to 1½ pt (900 ml) with milk. Grate cheese.

6 Melt margarine in dried potato pan. Stir in flour then gradually stir in milk and bring to the boil, stirring until thickened and smooth. Stir in nutmeg and plenty of salt and pepper.

89

7 Arrange half the potatoes in the base of eight individual heatproof dishes then add the fish, leeks and half the cheese.

8 Spoon a little of the sauce over the cheese then top with overlapping slices of potato. Pour remaining sauce over to cover potatoes then sprinkle with cheese.

To serve now: *cook in a preheated oven set to 400°F, 200°C, Gas 6 for 40 minutes until browned.*

To freeze: *cool completely. Open-freeze until solid then cover with a lid or cling film. Seal, label and freeze for 1 month.*

To defrost: *take out as many portions as required and defrost for 4 hours at room temperature. Remove wrapping or lid and cook as To serve now.*

To microwave: *cover microproof dish with pierced cling film and cook one portion at a time on defrost (30 per cent) for 10 minutes then full power for 3 minutes. Remove cling film and brown under a hot grill.*

Jumbalaya

Shopping tip Shop around for best priced bags of frozen fish.

Serves 8   Costs £££

2 onions

1 lb (450 g) courgettes

2 tbsp oil

1 lb (450 g) long grain white rice

2 tsp paprika

2 cloves garlic, crushed

2½ pt (1.5 litre) vegetable stock

2 bay leaves

3 tbsp lemon juice

3 tbsp tomato purée

1½ lb (675 g) bag frozen coley or hake fillets

Expert tip If rice appears to be drying out too quickly, then top up with boiling water.

Serving tip Sprinkle with a little frozen chopped parsley if available.

I Peel and finely chop the onions. Trim and dice courgettes.

2 Heat oil in a large saucepan or wok and fry the onion for 5 minutes, stirring until lightly browned. Add the courgettes and fry for 2 minutes.

3 Add the rice, paprika and garlic and fry for 2 minutes. Add the stock, bay leaves, lemon juice, tomato purée and plenty of salt and pepper and bring to the boil, stirring.

4 Peel skin off the frozen fish fillets. Add to pan, cover and simmer for 20 minutes, stirring rice occasionally until rice is tender and stock absorbed.

5 Break fish into chunky pieces carefully removing any bones. Spoon into individual ovenproof china or foil dishes.

To serve now: *serve immediately.*

To freeze: *cover with cling film or foil, seal and leave to cool completely. Label and freeze for 2–3 months.*

To defrost: *take out as many portions as required and defrost for 5 hours at room temperature. Cover with foil and cook at 400°F, 200°C, Gas 6 for 30 minutes until piping hot.*

To microwave: *cook one portion at a time in a micro-proof dish, covered with pierced cling film on defrost (30 per cent) for 10 minutes. Stir and cook on full power for 2 minutes. Stir before serving.*

SLOW COOK CASSEROLES

Country beef and dumplings
Peppered beef with prunes
Moroccan mince
Italian beef and olives
Chicken and spinach curry
Chicken purses
Chicken nicoise
Pork and red cabbage casserole
Pork and pumpkin casserole
Tuscan pork and bean stew
Braised lamb with lemon and parsnips
Spicy baked hearts
Spiced vegetable tagine
Parsnip cassoulet
Aubergine layer

Country beef and dumplings

Shopping tip Shop around for stewing beef – it varies considerably in price and quality. Avoid expensive ready diced beef.

Ingredients tip Dijon mustard is quite mild; substitute coarse grain mustard or 1 tsp English mustard.

Cooking tip Cook casserole in a deep roasting tin covered with foil or an upturned baking sheet if your casserole dishes aren't big enough.

Serves 8　　Costs £££

2 lb (900 g) stewing beef

2 onions

1½ lb (675 g) carrots

1½ lb (675 g) swede

2 tbsp oil

2 lb (900 g) potatoes

2 tbsp plain flour

2½ pt (1.5 litre) beef stock

1 tbsp Dijon mustard

2 tbsp Worcestershire sauce

2 tsp mixed dried herbs

Dumplings

12 oz (350 g) self-raising flour

6 oz (150 g) shredded suet

1 tsp mixed dried herbs

---

1 Preheat the oven to 350°F, 180°C, Gas 4. Trim any fat from beef and cut meat into cubes. Peel and chop onion. Peel and dice carrot and swede.

2 Heat oil in a large saucepan or wok, add beef in small batches and fry, stirring until evenly browned. Drain and transfer to a large casserole dish.

3 Fry onion until lightly browned. Add carrots and swede and fry for 2 minutes, stirring.

4 Peel potatoes and cut into large chunks, add to pan and fry for 2 minutes.

5 Stir in flour then add stock, mustard, Worcestershire sauce, herbs and plenty of salt and pepper. Bring to the boil, stirring.

93

Freezing tip If planning to defrost portion in the microwave, freeze food in a plastic bag or microproof dish.

6 Pour over beef. Cover and transfer to the oven. Cook for 1½ hours or until beef is tender.

7 Put dumpling ingredients into a bowl with plenty of salt and pepper. Mix to a soft but not sticky dough with 6–7 fl oz (175–200 ml) cold water. Cut into 16 and shape into small balls with floured hands.

To serve now: *add dumplings to hot casserole. Recover and cook in the oven for a further 30 minutes until dumplings are well risen and fluffy. Spoon into soup bowls and serve with frozen peas.*

To freeze: *cool casserole completely. Open-freeze dumplings on a baking sheet until hard then pack into a plastic box, interleaving layers with foil. Pack casserole into small bags. Seal, label and freeze for 4–6 months.*

To defrost: *take out as many portions of casserole as required, put bags into a saucepan. Defrost for 5 hours at room temperature. Remove bags, bring to the boil, add as many dumplings as required. Cover and simmer for 20 minutes, or until dumplings are completely cooked. Topping up with extra stock if needed.*

To microwave: *remove casserole from bag and put one portion in a microproof serving dish, cover with cling film and cook on defrost (30 per cent) for 15 minutes. Stir, recover and cook on full power for 1 minute. Add 2 still frozen dumplings, recover and cook for 5–6 minutes or until dumplings are completely cooked.*

Peppered beef with prunes

Ingredients tip If you don't have a pestle and mortar then put peppercorns in a mug and crush with the end of a rolling pin.

Expert tip For a special occasion, substitute some of the stock for wine or beer.

Cooking method Cooks well in a slow cooker: see handbook for timings.

Serves 8   Costs £££

2 lb (900 g) stewing beef

3 onions

1¼ lb (550 g) carrots

1 head of celery

2 tbsp oil

3 cloves garlic, crushed

2 tbsp plain flour

1½ pt (900 ml) beef stock

1 tbsp brown sugar

small bunch fresh rosemary or 1 tsp dried

2 tsp black peppercorns

4 oz (100 g) ready to eat stoned prunes

---

1 Preheat the oven to 350°F, 180°C, Gas 4. Trim fat from beef and cut meat into cubes.

2 Peel and chop onion. Peel carrots, cut in half lengthways then into slices. Trim, wash and slice celery.

3 Heat oil in large saucepan or wok, add beef in small batches and fry, stirring until evenly browned. Drain and transfer to a large casserole dish.

4 Fry onion until lightly browned. Add carrots, celery and garlic and fry for 2 minutes, stirring.

5 Stir in flour then add stock, sugar, rosemary and salt. Crush peppercorns coarsely with a pestle and mortar. Halve prunes. Add pepper and prunes to casserole.

6 Bring to the boil, stirring, then pour into casserole. Cover and transfer to the oven. Cook for 2 hours or until beef is tender.

To serve now: spoon on to plates and serve with mashed potatoes and peas.

To freeze: cool casserole completely. Spoon into small plastic bags. Seal, label and freeze for 4–6 months.

To defrost: take out as many portions as required, put bags into a saucepan. Defrost for 5 hours at room temperature. Remove bags, cover pan, bring to boil slowly then boil for 5 minutes.

To microwave: remove metal tag and put one portion in a microproof serving dish. Cook on defrost (30 per cent) for 10 minutes. Remove bag and use to loosely cover dish. Cook on full power for 3 minutes. Stir well before serving.

Moroccan mince

Serving tip Serve with cous cous, rice or mashed potato.

Ingredients tip Although there seem to be a lot of spices, finished dish is mellow and surprisingly mild. Add more garlic for garlic fans.

Serves 8   Costs ££

1 onion

1 lb (450 g) minced beef or lamb

8 oz (225 g) carrot

8 oz (225 g) parsnip

2 cloves garlic, crushed

4 oz (100 g) green lentils

15 oz (420 g) can chick peas

14 oz (400 g) can tomatoes

1 tbsp tomato purée

1 tsp turmeric

2 tsp ground ginger

2 tsp ground cinnamon

3 tsp ground coriander

1¼ pt (750 ml) chicken stock

3 oz (75 g) ready to eat stoned prunes

3 oz (75 g) sultanas

Healthy tip Adding lentils, pulses and lots of vegetables stretches mince and adds fibre.

1. Preheat the oven to 350°F, 180°C, Gas 4. Chop onion and dry fry with mince in a large saucepan or wok, stirring until mince is evenly browned.

2. Peel and dice carrots and parsnips. Add to mince with garlic and fry for 2–3 minutes, stirring.

3. Stir in lentils, drained chick peas, tomatoes, tomato purée, spices and stock.

4. Roughly chop prunes and stir into mince with sultanas and plenty of salt and pepper. Bring to the boil then transfer to a large casserole dish. Cover and cook in the oven for 1¼ hours.

To serve now: *spoon on to plates.*

To freeze: *cool completely. Spoon portions into small plastic bags, seal, label and freeze for 4–6 months.*

To defrost: *take out as many portions as required, put bags into a saucepan. Defrost for 4 hours at room temperature. Remove bag, cover pan and bring to the boil slowly. Boil for 5 minutes.*

To microwave: *remove metal tag from bag and microwave one portion at a time in a microproof serving dish on defrost (30 per cent) for 10 minutes. Take out of bag, use to loosely cover dish, cook on full power for 2 minutes. Stir before serving.*

Italian beef and olives

Ingredients tip Vary the vegetables, add mushrooms, and green pepper if preferred. Can also use lamb mince

Cooking tip Use a large flameproof dish, if you have one, for frying and cooking – saves on washing up.

Serving tip Serve with rice or pasta.

Serves 8   **Costs £££**

2 onions

12 oz (350 g) courgettes

1 red pepper

2 lb (900 g) minced beef

2 cloves garlic, crushed

1 tbsp plain flour

1¾ lb (800 g) can tomatoes

small bunch fresh thyme or 1 tsp dried

2 tsp sugar

3 oz (75 g) drained stuffed green olives

---

1 Preheat the oven to 350°F, 180°C, Gas 4. Peel and chop the onions. Trim and dice courgettes. Halve, core and deseed pepper then dice.

2 Dry fry onion and mince in a large saucepan, stirring until mince is evenly browned.

3 Add courgettes, pepper and garlic and fry for 2 minutes, stirring.

4 Stir in flour then add tomatoes, thyme, sugar and plenty of salt and pepper. Bring to the boil, breaking up the tomatoes.

5 Slice the olives and add to mince. Spoon into a large casserole dish, cover and transfer to the oven. Cook for 1¼ hours.

To serve now: spoon on to plates.

To freeze: cool completely. Spoon into small plastic bags. Seal, label and freeze for 4–6 months.

To defrost: take out as many bags as required, put into a saucepan. Defrost for 4 hours at room temperature. Remove bags, cover *and bring to boil slowly then boil for 5 minutes.*

To microwave: remove metal tag from bag, put in a microproof serving dish and cook one portion at a time on defrost (30 per cent) for 10 minutes. Take out of bag, use to loosely cover dish and cook on full power for 2½ minutes. Stir before serving.

Chicken and spinach curry

Serving tip Cooking chicken with lots of vegetables helps to extend the meat, but if cooking for hungry men or teenage boys you may need to serve two pieces of chicken each.

Freezing tip Tie bag of rice and bag of chicken together so that they are easy to find in the freezer.

Serves 8   Costs ££

2 lb 14 oz (1.3 kg) frozen chicken thighs, defrosted

1 tbsp oil

1 onion

8 oz (225 g) carrots

8 oz (225 g) parsnips

4 tbsp medium curry powder

4 oz (100 g) red lentils

1 pt (600 ml) chicken stock

4 oz (100 g) frozen leaf spinach

To serve

1 lb (450 g) long grain rice

I Preheat the oven to 350°F, 180°C, Gas 4. Rinse chicken with cold water, drain, dry with kitchen paper. Trim skin if needed.

2 Heat oil in a large saucepan, add chicken and fry until browned. Drain and transfer to a large casserole dish

3 Peel and chop onion, carrots and parsnips. Add vegetables; fry, stirring, until lightly softened.

4 Stir in curry powder, cook for 1 minute. Add lentils and stock, season well with salt and pepper and bring to the boil.

99

5 Transfer to a casserole dish, cover and cook in the oven for 1 hour. Add frozen spinach and recover dish.

6 Just before end of cooking, cook rice in a saucepan of boiling salted water for 8–10 minutes. Drain and rinse with hot water.

To serve now: return casserole dish to oven and cook for 15 minutes until spinach is hot. Keep drained rice hot in pan.

To freeze: cool completely. Pack portions of chicken and rice into separate plastic bags. Seal, label and freeze for 2–3 months.

To defrost: defrost a portion of rice and chicken on a plate for 4 hours at room temperature. Take chicken out of bag, put into a saucepan, cover and bring slowly to the boil. Boil for 5 minutes. Plunge rice into a pan of boiling water. Cook for 3 minutes. Drain and serve with chicken.

To microwave: remove metal tag from bags. Cook one portion of chicken in bag on a micro-proof serving plate on defrost (30 per cent) for 10 minutes. Cook rice in bag on full power for 2 minutes. Take chicken out of bag, put on plate, loosely cover with bag and cook for 3 minutes on full power. Spoon rice around chicken, cook for 1 minute.

Chicken purses

Shopping tip If short of time make up half the quantity so there is less fiddly boning to do.

Ingredients tip Add 2 cloves crushed garlic if liked.

Cooking tip Boning and stuffing the drumsticks adds flavour and makes this humble joint into something special.

Serving suggestion Don't forget to remove the cocktail sticks. Serve with celeriac and potato purée, p120 and steamed brussel sprouts.

Serves 8   Costs £££

4 lb (1.8 kg) or 16 chicken drumsticks, defrosted if frozen

4 rashers streaky bacon

2 onions

4 oz (100 g) button mushrooms

2 tbsp oil

4 oz (100 g) breadcrumbs

1 oz (25 g) soft margarine

2 tbsp plain flour

1½ pt (900 ml) chicken stock

small bunch fresh rosemary or 1 tsp dried

I Preheat the oven to 350°F, 180°C, Gas 4. Rinse chicken with cold water, drain well and put on to a baking sheet.

2 Bone each drumstick by inserting a small knife between bone and meat at thickest part of drumstick. Stand drumstick on end and work down the bone, scraping the meat away until the base is reached. Pull skin over base of bone then cut to release bone. Reshape drumstick so skin is outside.

3 Cut rind away from bacon, then finely chop bacon and onion. Wipe and chop mushrooms.

4 Heat oil in a frying pan, add bacon and onion and fry, stirring until golden. Add mushrooms and fry for 2 minutes. Stir in breadcrumbs and plenty of salt and pepper. Cool slightly.

5 Press spoonfuls of mixture inside each drumstick. Secure ends with cocktail sticks.

6 Heat margarine in a large frying pan, fry

chicken in batches until browned on all sides. Drain and transfer to a large casserole dish.

7 Stir flour into pan juices then gradually stir in stock and bring to the boil, stirring until thickened and smooth. Add rosemary and plenty of salt and pepper. Pour over the chicken.

8 Cover and transfer to the oven. Cook for 1 hour. Remove cocktail sticks.

To serve now: spoon on to plates.

To freeze: cool completely. Pack into individual dishes or plastic bags. Seal, label and freeze for 2–3 months.

To defrost: defrost as many portions as required for 4 hours at room temperature. Reheat in individual ovenproof dishes, covered with foil in a preset oven 400°F, 200°C, Gas 6 for 30 minutes until piping hot.

To microwave: put one portion in a microproof serving dish, cover with pierced cling film. Cook on defrost(30 per cent) for 10 minutes then full power for 8 minutes.

Chicken nicoise

Shopping tip Look out for special offer bags of small multi-coloured peppers or buy three different coloured peppers from your local street market.

Serves 8   Costs £££

8 chicken pieces, defrosted if frozen

2 tbsp oil

2 onions

1 lb 2 oz (500 g) bag small coloured peppers

3 cloves garlic, crushed

1 tbsp plain flour

1¾ lb (800 g) can tomatoes

½ pt (300 ml) chicken stock

1 tsp sugar

few sprigs of fresh thyme or 1 tsp dried

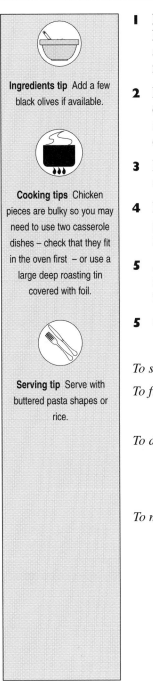

1 Preheat the oven to 350°F, 180°C, Gas 4. Rinse chicken pieces with cold water, drain and dry with kitchen paper. Trim skin if needed.

2 Heat oil in a large frying pan and fry chicken in batches until browned on both sides. Drain and transfer to a large casserole dish.

3 Peel and slice onions. Rinse peppers, halve, scoop out core and seeds, then thinly slice.

4 Fry onion until golden. Add peppers and garlic and fry for 2 minutes, stirring then add flour.

5 Add remaining ingredients and plenty of salt and pepper. Bring to the boil, stirring then pour over the chicken.

5 Cover and transfer to the oven and cook for 1¼ hours.

To serve now: *spoon on to serving plates.*

To freeze: *cool completely then pack into small plastic bags. Seal, label and freeze for 4–6 months.*

To defrost: *take out as many portions as required, put bags in a saucepan. Defrost for 5 hours at room temperature. Remove bags, cover and slowly bring to the boil. Boil for 5 minutes.*

To microwave: *remove metal tag, put bag in a microproof serving dish, cook one portion at a time on defrost (30 per cent) for 15 minutes. Take out of bag, loosely cover dish with bag and cook on full power for 3 minutes.*

Pork and red cabbage casserole

Shopping tip If spare rib chops are very large, buy four and cut in half.

Ingredients tip The high quantity of sugar and vinegar gives a sweet and sour taste to the finished dish. Use brown or white sugar, red or white wine vinegar.

Cooking tip You may need to cook in two dishes or a large roasting tin — check that they will fit in the oven before filling.

Serves 8   Costs £££

1½ lb (675 g) red cabbage

2 tbsp oil

8 spare rib pork chops or shoulder steaks

2 onions

1 lb (450 g) cooking apples

2 tbsp plain flour

1½ pt (900 ml) chicken stock

6 tbsp soft light brown sugar

6 tbsp wine vinegar

2 tbsp tomato purée

2 tsp Dijon mustard

I Preheat the oven to 350°F, 180°C, Gas 4. Finely slice the red cabbage discarding the woody core and put into a large shallow ovenproof dish.

2 Heat the oil in a large frying pan, fry the pork in batches until browned on both sides. Drain and arrange on top of the cabbage.

3 Peel and chop the onion then fry in the pan juices until golden. Quarter, core, peel and slice apple. Add to pan and cook for 2 minutes.

4 Stir in the flour then add the stock, sugar, vinegar, tomato purée, mustard and plenty of salt and pepper. Bring to the boil then pour over the pork.

5 Cover and transfer to the oven. Cook for 1½ hours or until pork is tender.

To serve now: *spoon on to serving plates.*

To freeze: *cool completely. Pack into small plastic bags. Seal, label and freeze for 2–3 months.*

To defrost: *take out as many portions as required, put into an ovenproof dish. Defrost for 4 hours at room temperature. Remove bags, cover dish with foil and cook at 375°F, 190°C, Gas 5 for 30 minutes.*

To microwave: *remove metal tag from bag, put on a microproof plate and cook one portion at a time on defrost (30 per cent) for 10 minutes. Remove bag, cover plate loosely with bag and cook on full power for 4 minutes.*

Serving tip Sprinkle with a little chopped frozen parsley. Serve with mashed potatoes and frozen green beans.

Pork and pumpkin casserole

Ingredients tip Pumpkins are often used only for lanterns and pies. Buy a large wedge rather than a small pumpkin as there is less waste.

Shopping tip Buy pork spare rib chops if cheaper; prices vary.

Serving tip Serve with potatoes and peas.

Serves 8   Costs £££

3 tbsp oil

8 spare rib pork chops or shoulder steaks

2 onions

2 lb (900 g) pumpkin

2 tsp ground ginger

1 tsp ground cinnamon

1 tsp turmeric

2 tbsp plain flour

1½ pt (900 ml) chicken stock

2 tbsp brown sugar

I Preheat the oven to 350°F, 180°C, Gas 4. Heat oil in a large frying pan or wok and fry pork in batches until browned on both sides. Drain and transfer to a large casserole dish.

2 Peel and chop onion, fry in pan juices until softened.

3 Meanwhile, cut pumpkin into thick slices, scoop out seeds and cut away peel. Cut into large dice. Fry for 2 minutes, stirring.

4 Stir spices and flour into vegetables. Add

stock, sugar and plenty of salt and pepper. Bring to the boil then pour over pork.

5 Cover and cook in the oven for 1½ hours.

To serve now: *spoon on to plates and serve with mashed potatoes and peas.*

To freeze: *cool completely. Pack portions into small plastic bags. Seal, label and freeze for 2–3 months.*

To defrost: *take out as many portions as required, put into an ovenproof dish. Defrost for 4 hours at room temperature. Remove bags, cover dish with foil and cook at 375°F, 190°C, Gas 5 for 30 minutes.*

To microwave: *remove metal tag, put bag on a micro-proof plate. Cook one portion at a time on defrost (30 per cent) for 10 minutes. Remove bag, use to loosely cover plate and cook on full power for 4 minutes.*

Tuscan pork and bean stew

Healthy tip Very high in fibre.

Serving tip A complete meal. Could serve with crusty bread or garlic bread.

Serves 8   Costs £££

12 oz (350 g) mixed dried beans, soaked overnight in cold water

2½ lb (1.1 kg) lean belly pork rashers

2 onions

1 lb (450 g) carrots

1 lb (450 g) courgettes

8 oz (225 g) button mushrooms

3 cloves garlic, crushed

1¾ lb (800 g) can tomatoes

¾ pt (450 ml) chicken stock

2 tbsp pesto

I   Drain beans, put in a saucepan, cover with cold water and bring to the boil. Boil rapidly

Shopping tip Pork rashers are very cheap. Choose those with the most meat.

for 10 minutes then simmer for 1 hour or until beans are tender. Drain.

2 Preheat the oven to 350°F, 180°C, Gas 4. Cut rind away from pork and slice. Peel and chop onions. Peel and dice carrots. Trim and slice courgettes. Halve mushrooms.

3 Dry fry pork and onion in a saucepan over a gentle heat until fat begins to run from pork. Increase heat and fry until lightly browned. Add carrots, courgettes, mushrooms and garlic and fry for 2 minutes, stirring.

4 Stir in tomatoes, stock, pesto and plenty of salt and pepper.

5 Transfer to a large casserole dish, add drained beans. Cover and cook in the oven for 1½ hours.

To serve: spoon into dishes.

To freeze: cool completely. Spoon portions into small plastic bags. Seal, label and freeze for 2–3 months.

To defrost: take out as many bags as required, put in a saucepan. Defrost for 4 hours at room temperature. Remove bags, cover pan and slowly bring to the boil. Boil for 5 minutes, stirring occasionally.

To microwave: remove metal tag from bag and microwave one portion at a time in a microproof serving dish on defrost (30 per cent) for 13 minutes. Remove bag and loosely cover pork. Cook on full power for 3 minutes. Stir before serving.

Braised lamb with lemon and parsnips

Shopping tip Depending on time of year fresh neck of lamb can be the same price as frozen. Fresh lamb is often cut into thicker meatier pieces.

Ingredients tip Lemon flavour is tangy and quite strong: use 1 lemon if preferred.

Serving tip Sprinkle with a little frozen parsley just before serving.

Serves 8   Costs £££

2 tbsp oil

3½ lb (1.6 kg) neck of lamb, defrosted if frozen

2 onions

1½ lb (675 g) parsnips

2 tbsp plain flour

1½ pt (900 ml) chicken stock

2 lemons

small bunch fresh sage or 1 tsp dried

---

1 Preheat the oven to 350°F, 180°C, Gas 4. Heat oil in a large saucepan and fry lamb in batches until browned on both sides. Drain and transfer to a large casserole dish or deep roasting tin.

2 Peel and chop onions, peel and dice parsnips. Fry onion in pan juices until softened. Add parsnips and fry for 2 minutes, stirring.

3 Stir in flour then add stock and plenty of salt and pepper. Slice lemons and add to pan with sage. Bring to the boil then transfer to casserole dish.

4 Cover and cook in the oven for 1¾ hours.

To serve now: *serve with mashed potatoes and steamed broccoli.*

To freeze: *cool completely. Pack portions into small plastic bags. Seal, label and freeze for 4–6 months.*

To defrost: *take out as many portions as required, put into a saucepan, still in bags. Defrost for 4 hours at room temperature. Remove bags, cover and bring slowly to the boil then boil for 5 minutes, stirring occasionally.*

To microwave: remove metal tag and put bag in a microproof dish, cook one portion at a time on defrost (30 per cent) for 10 minutes. Remove bag, use to cover dish loosely and cook on full power for 3 minutes.

Spicy baked hearts

Shopping tip Hearts are very often sold at knock down prices.

Ingredients tip For garlic fans add 3–4 cloves of crushed garlic. Use a mixture of nutmeg and cinnamon if you don't have any allspice.

Expert tip Many people are put off by the shape and idea of eating hearts, slicing helps to overcome this.

Serves 8   Costs £££

8 lambs' hearts

2 tbsp oil

2 onions

1 lb (450 g) carrots

8 oz (225 g) red lentils

1¾ lb (800 g) can tomatoes

1 pt (600 ml) lamb stock

2 tsp ground allspice

---

1 Preheat the oven to 350°F, 180°C, Gas 4. Rinse lambs' hearts with cold water and drain well. Cut into thick slices.

2 Heat oil in a large saucepan or wok and fry lamb in batches until browned on both sides. Drain and transfer to a large casserole dish.

3 Peel and chop onions. Peel and dice carrots. Add onions to pan and fry until lightly browned. Add carrots and fry for 2 minutes, stirring.

4 Add remaining ingredients and plenty of salt and pepper. Bring to the boil, breaking tomatoes up with a spoon. Pour over lamb.

5 Cover and transfer to the oven, cook for 2 hours or until lamb is tender.

To serve now: spoon on to plates and serve with steamed cous cous or rice.

109

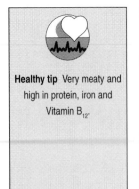

Healthy tip Very meaty and high in protein, iron and Vitamin B$_{12}$.

To freeze: cool completely. Spoon into small plastic bags. Seal, label and freeze for 3–4 months.

To defrost: take out as many portions as required and put into individual dishes. Defrost for 4 hours at room temperature. Remove bags, cover with foil and cook at 375°F, 190°C, Gas 5 for 35 minutes.

To microwave: remove metal tag, put bag on a microproof plate and cook on defrost (30 per cent) for 10 minutes. Remove bag, use to loosely cover dish and cook on full power for 3 minutes. Stir before serving.

Spiced vegetable tagine

Ingredients tip Vary the vegetables: a good way to use up the fridge ends.

Suitable for a vegetarian.

Health tip High in fibre.

Serves 8   Costs £

5 oz (125 g) dried haricot beans, soaked overnight in cold water

1 onion

12 oz (350 g) carrots

12 oz (350 g) courgettes

1 red pepper

1 tbsp oil

2 cloves garlic, crushed

14 oz (400 g) can tomatoes

4 oz (100 g) red lentils

¼ tsp grated nutmeg

½ tsp ground cinnamon

½ tsp ground ginger

5 cloves

¾ pt (450 ml) vegetable stock

I   Drain haricot beans, put in a saucepan with fresh cold water and bring to the boil. Boil rapidly for 10 minutes then reduce heat and simmer for 1 hour or until beans are tender.

2 Drain beans in a colander and set aside.

3 Preheat the oven to 350°F, 180°C, Gas 4. Peel and chop onion. Peel and dice carrots. Slice courgettes. Slice red pepper, discarding core and seeds.

4 Heat oil in a large saucepan, add onions and fry until golden. Add carrots, courgettes, red pepper and garlic and fry for 2 minutes.

5 Add tomatoes, lentils, spices, stock, cooked beans and plenty of salt and pepper. Bring to the boil, stirring.

6 Spoon into a large casserole dish, cover and transfer to the oven. Cook for 1 hour or until lentils are soft.

To serve now: *spoon into dishes.*

To freeze: *cool completely. Spoon into small plastic bags. Seal, label and freeze for 2–3 months.*

To defrost: *take out as many portions as required, put bags in a saucepan. Defrost for 4 hours at room temperature. Remove bags, cover and bring slowly to the boil then boil for 5 minutes, stirring occasionally.*

To microwave: *remove metal tag from bag, put in a microproof dish and cook one portion at a time on full power for 3 minutes. Remove bag and use to cover food, cook for 3 minutes more. Stir before serving.*

Parsnip cassoulet

Suitable for a vegetarian.

Ingredients tip Use 3 tbsp parmesan cheese instead of almonds if liked.

Serving tip Delicious served with hot garlic bread.

Healthy tip Very high in fibre.

Serves 8   Costs ££

1 lb 2 oz (500 g) pack country bean mix, soaked overnight in cold water

2 onions

2 lb (900 g) parsnips

2 tbsp oil

4 cloves garlic, crushed

1¾ lb (800 g) can tomatoes

1 tbsp tomato purée

¾ pt (450 ml) vegetable stock

1 tbsp sugar

2 oz (50 g) ground almonds

---

1 Drain beans, put in a saucepan with fresh cold water and bring to the boil. Boil rapidly for 10 minutes then reduce heat and simmer for 1 hour or until beans are tender.

2 Drain beans in a colander and set aside.

3 Preheat the oven to 350°F, 180°C, Gas 4. Peel and chop onions. Peel and dice parsnips.

4 Heat oil in a large saucepan or wok and fry onions until golden. Add parsnips and garlic and fry for 2 minutes, stirring.

5 Stir in beans, tomatoes, tomato purée, stock, sugar and plenty of salt and pepper. Bring to the boil, breaking up tomatoes with a spoon.

6 Transfer to a large casserole dish and sprinkle top with almonds. Cover and cook in the oven for 1 hour. Remove the lid and cook for 20 minutes or until browned.

To serve now: serve hot with salad.

To freeze: cool completely. Spoon into individual foil or china dishes. Cover with foil or cling film. Seal, label and freeze for 4–6 months.

To defrost: take out as many portions as required and defrost for 4 hours at room temperature. Cook foil covered dishes at 400°F, 200°C, Gas 6 for 35 minutes.

To microwave: cover microproof dish with pierced cling film. Cook one portion at a time on defrost (30 per cent) for 10 minutes then full power for 4 minutes.

Aubergine layer

Shopping tip Make this with bargain priced aubergines from your local market.

Ingredients tip Sprinkle top with parmesan if liked.

Serving tip Delicious served with hot garlic bread.

Serves 8   Costs ££

2 medium aubergines

5 tbsp oil

2 onions

2 cloves garlic, crushed

1¾ lb (800 g) can tomatoes

2 tsp sugar

small bunch fresh oregano or 1 tsp dried

7 oz (200 g) cheddar cheese

3 tbsp breadcrumbs

I Preheat the oven to 350°F, 180°C, Gas 4. Wash, trim and thinly slice the aubergines. Lay in a single layer on a large tray and sprinkle with salt. Leave to stand for 20 minutes.

2 Rinse aubergines slices with cold water, squeeze dry with hands and put on a clean tray.

3 Heat 2 tbsp oil in a wok or large frying pan, fry aubergine in batches until browned on

both sides. Add 1–2 tbsp more oil as needed. Drain aubergines well and reserve.

4 Peel and chop onions, fry in remaining oil until golden. Add garlic, tomatoes, sugar, oregano and plenty of salt and pepper. Bring to the boil, breaking up tomatoes with a spoon. Cook for 3 minutes.

5 Coarsely grate cheese. Arrange one third of the aubergines in the base of a rectangular ovenproof dish or small roasting tin. Add one third of the tomato mixture and one third of the cheese. Repeat layers ending with cheese.

6 Sprinkle with breadcrumbs and transfer to the oven. Cook uncovered for 1¼ hours until topping is golden.

To serve now: *serve hot with salad.*

To freeze: *cool completely. Cut into eight pieces and wrap each in foil. Seal, label and then pack portions into a large plastic bag. Freeze for 4–6 months.*

To defrost: *take out as many portions as required and put on a baking sheet. Defrost for 4 hours at room temperature. Loosen foil and cook at 400°F, 200°C, Gas 6 for 30 minutes.*

To microwave: *unwrap portion and put on a micro-proof plate, cover with pierced cling film. Cook one portion at a time on full power for 5 minutes. Leave to stand for 5 minutes before serving.*

SIDE DISHES

Citrus glazed carrots and swede

Saucy broad beans with bacon

Sweet and sour vegetables

Braised celery with mustard

Celeriac and potatoe purée

Tangy Mediterranean leeks

Potato and parsnip galette

Duchesse potatoes

Parmesan and potato croquettes

Pilau rice

Citrus glazed carrots and swede

Serves 8   Costs £

1½ lb (675 g) carrots

1½ lb (675 g) swede

2 oz (50 g) soft margarine

1 tbsp sugar

6 fl oz (175 ml) orange juice

1 Peel and dice carrots and swede. Cook in a saucepan of boiling water for 10 minutes until just tender.

2 Drain, dry pan and melt margarine. Return vegetables to pan with sugar, orange juice and salt and pepper then mix together well.

To serve now: *cook for 3–4 minutes, stirring occasionally then spoon into a serving dish.*

To freeze: *cool then pack into small plastic bags. Seal, label and freeze for 4–6 months.*

To defrost: *leave for 3 hours at room temperature. Take out of bag and reheat in a small saucepan for 3–4 minutes.*

To microwave: *remove bag and put one portion in a microproof serving dish. Loosely cover with bag and cook on full power for 3 minutes. Stir well before serving.*

Shopping tip Use orange juice from a carton of long life, or the juice from two oranges if preferred.

Ingredients tip Add 2 tbsp fresh chopped rosemary, chives, parsley or tarragon if available.

Suitable for a vegetarian.

116

Saucy broad beans with bacon

Ingredients tip If you have fresh herbs in the garden, add 2 tbsp fresh chopped tarragon, chives or parsley.

Expert tip You may need to add a little extra milk when reheating if sauce seems very thick.

Serves 8   Costs £

2 oz (50 g) streaky bacon

2 oz (50 g) soft margarine

2 oz (50 g) plain flour

1 pt (600 ml) milk

1½ lb (675 g) frozen broad beans

1 Cut rind away from bacon then cut into small pieces.

2 Heat margarine in a saucepan, add bacon and fry for 2 minutes. Stir in flour. Gradually stir in milk and bring to the boil, stirring until thickened and smooth.

3 Add broad beans and salt and pepper. Cover and simmer for 4–5 minutes, stirring occasionally until beans are cooked.

To serve now: spoon on to plates.

To freeze: cool completely. Spoon into small plastic bags. Seal, label and freeze for 1 month.

To defrost: leave for 3 hours at room temperature. Take out of bag and reheat beans in a small saucepan for 5 minutes, stirring occasionally.

To microwave: remove bag, put one portion in a microproof serving dish. Loosely cover with bag and cook on full power for 3 minutes. Stir well before serving.

Sweet and sour vegetables

Cooking tip Use a preserving pan if you have one.

Vegetarian tip Use vegetable stock.

Serves 8   Costs £

6 sticks of celery

1 lb (450 g) courgettes

1 lb (450 g) carrots

1 tbsp oil

4 tsp cornflour

4 tsp wine vinegar

4 tsp tomato ketchup

4 tsp sugar

4 tsp soy sauce

9 fl oz (250 ml) chicken stock

I Trim and wash celery. Trim courgettes, peel carrots. Cut vegetables into thin strips about 2 inch (5 cm) long.

2 Heat oil in a wok or large saucepan, add vegetables and stir fry for 3 minutes.

3 Put cornflour into a bowl, add vinegar, ketchup, sugar and soy sauce and mix together. Add to wok with stock, mix well and stir fry for 2 minutes.

To serve now: spoon on to plates.

To freeze: *cool completely. Spoon into small plastic bags. Seal, label and freeze for 2–3 months.*

To defrost: *take out as many bags as required and defrost for 3 hours at room temperature. Remove bags, reheat in a saucepan for 3–4 minutes.*

To microwave: *remove bag and put one portion in a microproof serving dish. Loosely cover with bag and cook on full power for 2 minutes. Stir well before serving.*

Braised celery with mustard

Serving tip Sprinkle with a little frozen chopped parsley just before serving. Delicious with roast pork or pork chops.

Vegetarian tip Suitable for a vegetarian if vegetable stock is used.

Serves 8   Costs £

2 heads of celery

2 oz (50 g) soft margarine

3 tbsp plain flour

1 pt (600 ml) chicken stock

3 tsp Dijon mustard

2 tbsp wine vinegar

2 tsp sugar

I Wash and trim celery then cut each stalk into 2 inch (5 cm) lengths.

2 Heat margarine in a saucepan, add celery and cook for 2 minutes. Stir in flour.

3 Gradually stir in stock and bring to the boil. Stir in mustard, vinegar, sugar and salt and pepper. Simmer, uncovered for 20 minutes, stirring occasionally until celery is tender.

To serve now: spoon on to plates.

To freeze: *cool completely. Spoon into small plastic bags. Seal, label and freeze for 2–3 months.*

To defrost: *take out as many bags as required and defrost for 3 hours at room temperature. Take out of bag and reheat in a saucepan for 5 minutes.*

To microwave: *remove bag, put one portion in a microproof serving dish. Loosely cover with bag and cook on full power for 2 minutes. Stir well before serving.*

119

Celeriac and potato purée

Serves 8   Costs £

1½ lb (675 g) celeriac

2 lb (900 g) potatoes

1 onion

2 oz (50 g) soft margarine

Shopping tip A medium sized celeriac should weigh about 1½ lb (675 g). Its strong celery taste mixes well with potato.

Freezing tip If you don't have any foil dishes then line ramekin dishes with cling film. Fill and freeze. Remove from dishes when solid.

Suitable for a vegetarian.

1 Peel and cut vegetables into small chunks. Put into a saucepan and just cover with water. Add salt and pepper and bring to the boil. Cover and simmer for about 20 minutes or until vegetables are tender.

2 Drain off water and reserve. Mash vegetables with margarine until creamy, adding a little cooking water if needed.

To serve now: *spoon on to plates.*

To freeze: *cool completely. Spoon into individual foil pudding dishes. Cover with foil. Seal, label and freeze for 4–6 months.*

To defrost: *leave for 4 hours at room temperature. Reheat in a preheated oven 400°F, 200°C, Gas 6 for 25 minutes still covered with foil. Stir well before serving.*

To microwave: *dip container in hot water, remove wrapping and dish. Put in a micro-proof dish, cover with pierced cling film and cook on full power for 3 minutes. Stir well before serving.*

Tangy Mediterranean leeks

Serving tip Delicious served with grilled mackerel or chicken.

Suitable for a vegetarian.

Serves 8   Costs £

1½ lb (675 g) leeks

1 tbsp oil

14 oz (400 g) can tomatoes

1 lemon, grated rind only

1 tbsp sugar

---

1 Trim and wash leeks well. Cut into thick slices.

2 Heat oil in a saucepan, add leeks and fry for 2 minutes. Add remaining ingredients and season with salt and pepper.

3 Bring to the boil, cover and simmer for 5 minutes.

To serve now: uncover pan and cook over a high heat for 2–3 minutes until sauce has thickened. Serve hot.

To freeze: cool completely. Spoon into small plastic bags. Seal, label and freeze for 4–6 months.

To defrost: take out as many bags as required and defrost for 3 hours at room temperature. Take out of bags and put into a saucepan. Cook for 4–5 minutes until hot.

To microwave: remove bag and put one portion in a microproof serving dish. Loosely cover with bag and cook on full power for 3 minutes. Stir well before serving.

121

Potato and parsnip galette

Serves 8   Costs £

2 lb (900 g) potatoes

1 lb (450 g) parsnips

1 oz (25 g) soft margarine

¼ tsp ground nutmeg

4 tsp cornflour

¾ pt (450 ml) milk

2 cloves garlic, crushed

---

1   Preheat the oven to 400°F, 200°C, Gas 6. Put a large saucepan of water on to boil. Peel and thinly slice the potatoes and parsnips. Add to pan, bring water back to the boil and cook for 3 minutes until almost tender.

2   Drain vegetables. Grease a 7 × 11 inch (18 × 28 cm) roasting tin with a little of the margarine then layer vegetables in tin with salt, pepper and nutmeg.

3   Mix cornflour to a paste with a little of the milk. Stir in remaining milk and garlic then pour over vegetables. Dot with remaining margarine.

4   Cook for 1¼ hours until browned and milk has almost all been absorbed.

To serve now: *spoon on to plates.*

To freeze: *cool completely. Cut into eight portions and wrap each portion in foil. Seal, label and freeze for 1 month.*

To defrost: *take out as many portions as required and defrost for 3 hours at room temperature. Open out foil so top of portion is exposed, put on a baking sheet and cook at 400°F, 200°C, Gas 6 for 20 minutes.*

To microwave: remove foil and put one portion on a microproof plate, cover with pierced cling film and cook on full power for 2½ minutes.

Duchesse potatoes

Uses store cupboard ingredients.

Expert tip Although sieving potato seems tiresome it makes piping effortless. Leave potato to cool slightly before piping or bag will be too hot to hold.

Method tip If you don't have a piping bag then spoon potato on to baking sheet and sprinkle with a little grated cheese or sesame seeds.

Suitable for a vegetarian.

Serves 8   Costs £

2 lb (900 g) potatoes

1 oz (25 g) soft margarine

2 eggs, size 3

---

1 Peel and cut potatoes into chunky pieces. Cook in a saucepan of boiling water until tender. Line a baking sheet with a large piece of foil and grease with a little of the margarine.

2 Drain potatoes and mash with remaining margarine until creamy. Then press through a sieve to remove any small lumps.

3 Beat eggs with plenty of salt and pepper then beat into potatoes.

4 Spoon into a large nylon piping bag fitted with a large star tube then pipe 24 whirls on to foil.

To serve: *preheat oven to 400°F, 200°C, Gas 6. Cook potato for 12–15 minutes until golden.*

To freeze: *open freeze on tray until solid. Peel off foil and layer in plastic box, interleaving layers with foil. Cover, seal, label and freeze for 4–6 months.*

To defrost: *put as many whirls of potato as required on a greased baking sheet and cook in a preheated oven 400°F, 200°C, Gas 6 for 15 minutes.*

Parmesan and potato croquettes

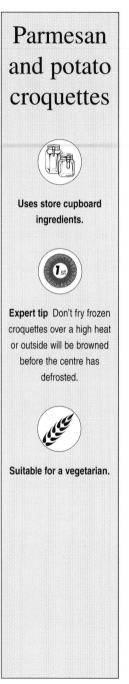

Uses store cupboard ingredients.

Expert tip Don't fry frozen croquettes over a high heat or outside will be browned before the centre has defrosted.

Suitable for a vegetarian.

Serves 8   Costs £

2 lb (900 g) potatoes
1 oz (25 g) soft margarine
6 tbsp milk
1 egg, size 3
2 oz (50 g) breadcrumbs
3 tbsp grated parmesan cheese
oil for frying

1 Peel and cut potatoes into chunky pieces. Cook in a saucepan of boiling water until tender.

2 Drain and mash with margarine, half the milk and salt and pepper.

3 Spoon potato into 16 mounds on a chopping board. Cool slightly then shape into thick sausages each about 3 inch (7.5 cm) long.

4 Mix remaining milk and egg on a plate. Put breadcrumbs and parmesan on a second plate.

5 Dip each croquette in egg then breadcrumbs and put on a baking sheet.

To serve now: *heat a little oil in the base of a large frying pan. Cook croquettes in batches, turning until golden and piping hot.*

To freeze: *open-freeze until solid. Remove from baking sheet and pack into a plastic box, interleaving layers with foil. Seal, label and freeze for 1 month.*

To defrost: *fry as many as required from frozen, in a covered pan, over a moderate heat for 8–10 minutes.*

124

Pilau rice

Expert tip Top up rice with a little extra boiling water towards end of cooking if rice is sticking. Rinse cold rice with a little boiling water if sticky.

Serving tip Serve with Chicken and spinach curry p99.

Suitable for a vegetarian.

Serves 8   Costs £

8 cardamom pods

1 tbsp oil

8 cloves

2 bay leaves

1 dried chilli, optional

1 lb (450 g) long grain white rice

¼ tsp turmeric

I Crush cardamom pods with a rolling pin. Heat oil in a large saucepan and add cardamom pods and any black seeds, cloves, bay leaves and chilli if using. Cook for 1 minute.

2 Add rice, turmeric and 2 pt (1.1 litre) water. Stir in salt and pepper and bring to the boil. Half cover pan with a lid then simmer for 10 minutes, stirring occasionally until rice is tender and water absorbed. Scoop out seeds and bay leaf with a fork.

To serve now: fluff up rice with a fork and spoon on to plates.

To freeze: cool completely. Fluff up rice with a fork. Spoon into small plastic bags. Seal, label and freeze for 2–3 months.

To defrost: take out as many portions as required, remove bags and put in a sieve or steamer, set above a pan of boiling water. Cover and steam for 5–8 minutes, stirring twice.

To microwave: remove bag, put one portion in a microproof serving dish. Loosely cover with bag and cook on full power for 2 minutes. Stir well before serving.

SAUCES

Barbecue sauce

Beef ragu

Carrot, tomato and pesto sauce

Mushroom and ham sauce

Herb sauce

Onion and mustard sauce

Speedy melba sauce

Tangy lemon sauce

Chocolate sauce

Cheat's custard

Barbecue sauce

Serves 8   Costs £

2 medium onions

1 lb (450 g) cooking apples

1 tbsp oil

2 tbsp cornflour

2 tbsp Worcestershire sauce

2 tbsp wine vinegar

2 tbsp brown sugar

2 tbsp tomato purée

1 pt (600 ml) chicken stock

Quick to make.

Ingredients tip A good way to use up windfall apples.

Vegetarian tip Use vegetable stock in place of chicken stock.

1 Peel and finely chop onions. Quarter, core, peel and finely chop apples.

2 Heat oil in a saucepan, add onions and apples and fry for 5 minutes, stirring until softened.

3 Put cornflour, Worcestershire sauce, vinegar, brown sugar and tomato purée into a small bowl and mix together until smooth.

4 Stir stock and cornflour mixture into pan, bring to the boil, stirring then simmer for 5 minutes.

To serve now: serve with grilled pork chops or
                   sausages.

To freeze: cool completely. Spoon into small
                   plastic bags. Seal, label and freeze for
                   2–3 months.

To defrost: put as many portions as required, still
                   in bags into a saucepan. Defrost for 2
                   hours at room temperature. Remove
                   bags and reheat, stirring until hot.

To microwave: remove bag and put one portion into a
                 small microproof dish. Cook on full
                 power for $2\frac{1}{2}$ minutes. Stir once dur-
                 ing cooking and just before serving.

127

Beef ragu

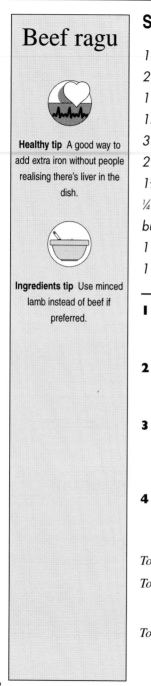

Healthy tip A good way to add extra iron without people realising there's liver in the dish.

Ingredients tip Use minced lamb instead of beef if preferred.

Serves 8   Costs ££

12 oz (350 g) lambs' liver, defrosted if frozen

2 onions

1 tbsp oil

1lb (450 g) minced beef

3 cloves garlic, crushed

2 tbsp plain flour

1¾ lb (800 g) can tomatoes

¼ pt (150 ml) beef stock

bunch fresh mixed herbs or 1 tsp dried oregano

1 tsp ground cinnamon

1 tbsp sugar

---

1 Rinse liver with cold water, drain well then roughly chop. Mince or finely chop in a food processor.

2 Peel and chop onions. Heat oil in a large saucepan, add the liver, onions and minced beef. Fry, stirring until mince is browned.

3 Stir in garlic and flour. Add tomatoes, stock, herbs, cinnamon, sugar and plenty of salt and pepper. Bring to the boil, breaking up tomatoes.

4 Cover and simmer for 45 minutes, stirring occasionally. Uncover and simmer for 15 minutes.

To serve now: *spoon on to a bed of cooked spaghetti.*

To freeze: *cool completely. Spoon into small plastic bags. Seal, label and freeze for 3–4 months.*

To defrost: *place portions, still in bags in a saucepan. Defrost for 4 hours at room temperature. Remove bags, bring to boil and cook for 5 minutes, stirring.*

To microwave: remove bag, put one portion into a microproof bowl. Loosely cover with bag and cook on defrost (30 per cent) for 5 minutes. Stir and cook on full power for 2 minutes. Stir well just before serving.

Carrot, tomato and pesto sauce

Serves 8   **Costs £**

2 medium onions

1 lb (450 g) carrots

1 tbsp oil

3 cloves garlic, crushed

1¾ lb (800 g) can tomatoes

1 tbsp sugar

2 tbsp pesto

Uses store cupboard ingredients.

Quick to make.

Suitable for a vegetarian.

1 Peel and finely chop onions. Peel and dice carrots.

2 Heat oil in a large saucepan and fry onion for 5 minutes, stirring until softened. Add carrots and garlic and cook for 2 minutes.

3 Add tomatoes, sugar and plenty of salt and pepper. Bring to the boil, breaking up the tomatoes then simmer, uncovered for 20 minutes, stirring occasionally.

4 Remove from heat and stir in the pesto.

To serve now: mix with cooked pasta and sprinkle with grated cheese. Allow 2 oz (50 g) dried pasta per portion.

To freeze: cool completely. Spoon into small plastic bags. Seal, label and freeze for 4–6 months.

To defrost: put as many portions as required, still in bags into a saucepan. Defrost for 2 hours at room temperature. Remove bags, reheat, stirring until hot.

To microwave: remove bag and put one portion into a microproof dish. Cook on full power for 2½ minutes. Stir once during cooking and just before serving.

Mushroom and ham sauce

Quick to make.

Vegetarian tip. Omit the ham and use vegetable stock.

Expert tip Allow 2 oz (50 g) dried pasta per person to serve with sauce.

Cooking method Use level spoon measures for flour or sauce will be too thick.

Serves 8   Costs ££

1 onion

1 lb (450 g) button mushrooms

2 tbsp oil

3 oz (75 g) soft margarine

4 tbsp plain flour

1 pt (600 ml) milk

½ pt (300 ml) chicken stock

4 oz (100 g) cheddar cheese

2 oz (50 g) wafer thin sliced ham

---

1 Peel and finely chop onion. Wipe and slice mushrooms.

2 Heat oil in a saucepan, add onion and fry for 5 minutes until lightly browned.

3 Add margarine and mushrooms and fry for 2–3 minutes, stirring.

4 Stir in flour then gradually add milk and stock. Bring to the boil, stirring until thickened.

5 Grate cheese, chop ham and stir both into sauce with plenty of salt and pepper. Cook for 2 minutes.

To serve now: serve on a bed of cooked pasta.

To freeze: cool completely. Spoon into small plastic bags. Seal, label and freeze for 1 month.

To defrost: put as many portions as required, still in bags into a saucepan, Defrost for

2 hours at room temperature. Remove bags, bring to the boil and cook for 3 minutes.

To microwave: remove bag, put one portion into a microproof bowl. Loosely cover with bag and cook on full power for 3 minutes. Stir once during cooking and just before serving.

Herb sauce

Quick to make.

Ingredients tip A good recipe to make if you have herbs growning in the garden. Use a mixture of parsley, chives, tarragon, and a little sage and rosemary. For a buttery sauce use half butter and half margarine.

Expert tip Add 2 tbsp dry vermouth, dry sherry or white wine if available for special occasions.

Serves 8   Costs £

1 onion
2 oz (50 g) fresh mixed herbs
4 oz (100 g) soft margarine
2 oz (50 g) plain flour
1 pt (600 ml) milk

---

1 Peel and roughly chop onion. Cook in a medium sized saucepan of boiling water for 3 minutes until softened. Drain and put into a liquidiser or food processor.

2 Take herbs off stems and add leaves to onion. Mix until very finely chopped. Add 2 oz (50 g) margarine and mix well.

3 Melt remaining margarine in dried onion pan. Stir in flour then gradually stir in milk. Bring to the boil, stirring until thickened and smooth.

4 Add herb butter and stir until well mixed. Season with salt and pepper.

To serve now: serve with grilled white fish or chicken.

To freeze: cool completely. Pack into two large ice cube trays and freeze until solid. Press cubes into a plastic bag, seal, label and freeze for 1 month.

To defrost: defrost four cubes per portion in a

Suitable for vegetarians

small saucepan for 2 hours at room temperature. Reheat, stirring until hot.

To microwave: put four cubes into a microproof jug, cook on full power for 1½ minutes. Stir once during cooking and just before serving.

Onion and mustard

Uses store cupboard ingredients.

Ingredients tip Stir in a little leftover or flat beer if available.

Expert tip Don't try to hurry cooking or the onions will burn and spoil the flavour.

Vegetarian tip Use vegetable stock in place of beef stock.

Serves 8   Costs £

1 lb 2 oz (500 g) onions

1 oz (25 g) soft margarine

1 tbsp oil

1 tbsp brown sugar

1 oz (25 g) plain flour

1¼ pt (750 ml) beef stock

3 tsp coarse grain or Dijon mustard

1 tbsp Worcestershire sauce

---

1 Peel, halve and thinly slice onions.

2 Heat margarine and oil in a large saucepan, add onions and fry gently for 20 minutes, stirring occasionally until softened.

3 Stir in sugar, increase the heat and fry for 20 minutes, stirring occasionally until onions are a rich brown.

4 Stir in flour then add stock, mustard, Worcestershire sauce and plenty of salt and pepper. Bring to the boil, stirring then simmer for 5 minutes.

To serve now: spoon over grilled sausages and serve with mashed potatoes and peas.

To freeze: cool completely. Pack into small plastic bags. Seal, label and freeze for 2–3 months.

To defrost: take out as many portions as required

Freezing tip You may need to stir in a little extra boiling water when reheating.

and defrost for 2 hours at room temperature. Transfer to a saucepan, and reheat, stirring until hot.

To microwave: remove bag and put one portion into a small microproof dish. Cook on full power for 2½ minutes. Stir once during cooking and just before serving.

Speedy melba sauce

Quick to make.

Uses store cupboard ingredients.

Serving tip For an easy peach melba, arrange two scoops of vanilla ice cream in a serving dish, add a few fresh or canned sliced peaches and pour hot sauce over. Decorate with mint from the garden.

Suitable for a vegetarian

Serves 8   Costs £

12 oz (340 g) jar strawberry jam

2 tbsp cornflour

½ pt (300 ml) orange juice from a carton

1 Put jam into a saucepan. Mix cornflour with a little orange juice until a smooth paste. Add to pan with remaining orange juice and ¼ pt (150 ml) water.

2 Bring mixture to the boil, stirring until thickened and smooth.

To serve now: spoon over scoops of ice cream or individual steamed puddings.

To freeze: cool completely. Pour into sections of two ice cube trays. Freeze until solid then press cubes into a plastic bag. Seal, label and freeze for 8–10 months.

To defrost: defrost four cubes per portion in a small saucepan for 2 hours at room temperature. Reheat, stirring until hot.

To microwave: put four cubes into a microproof jug, cook on full power for 1½ minutes. Stir once during cooking and just before serving.

Tangy lemon sauce

Quick to make.

Cooking tip Don't overheat eggs or they will curdle.

Expert tip Freeze remaining egg whites in a small plastic container for making meringues at a later date.

Freezing tip You may need to stir in a little boiling water when reheating sauce.

Serves 8   Costs £

1½ oz (40 g) cornflour

3 oz (75 g) caster sugar

2 lemons

2 egg yolks, size 3

1 Put cornflour and sugar into a bowl. Finely grate rind from lemons, then squeeze juice and stir into cornflour mixture until smooth.

2 Bring 1 pt (600 ml) water to the boil in a saucepan, gradually whisk into cornflour mixture and continue whisking until smooth.

3 Pour mixture into the saucepan and bring back to the boil, whisking continuously until thickened and sauce has cleared.

4 Take off the heat and beat in the egg yolks. Return to the heat and cook for 1 min, stirring.

To serve now: *serve with hot bread pudding, see p166 or warm slices of gingerbread or steamed pudding.*

To freeze: *cool completely. Pour into sections of two ice cube trays. Freeze until solid then press cubes into a plastic bag. Seal, label and freeze for 4–6 months.*

To defrost: *defrost four cubes per portion in a small saucepan for 2 hours at room temperature. Reheat, stirring until hot.*

To microwave: *put four cubes into a microproof jug, cook on full power for 2 minutes. Stir once during cooking and just before serving.*

134

Chocolate sauce

Serves 8   **Costs £**

3 oz (75 g) cocoa

3 oz (75 g) soft margarine

8 oz (225 g) granulated sugar

Serving tip This sauce is very rich, also good served with profiteroles for a special occasion.

Uses store cupboard ingredients.

Quick to make.

Suitable for a vegetarian.

1   Put cocoa into a saucepan, but do not put on the heat. Gradually whisk in ½ pt (300 ml) boiling water and whisk until smooth.

2   Add the margarine and sugar, cook over a medium heat, whisking occasionally until the sugar has dissolved and margarine has melted.

3   Boil for 3–4 minutes without stirring until sauce has thickened.

To serve now: *pour over fresh poached or canned pears.*

To freeze: *cool completely. Spoon into small plastic bags or individual plastic boxes. Seal, label and freeze for 4–6 months.*

To defrost: *put as many portions as required, still in bags into a saucepan. Defrost for 2 hours at room temperature. Remove containers. Reheat sauce, stirring until hot.*

To microwave: *remove bag and put one portion into a small microproof dish. Cook on full power for 1½ minutes. Stir once during cooking and just before serving.*

135

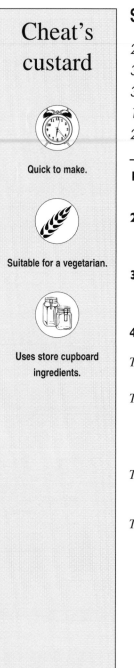

Cheat's custard

Quick to make.

Suitable for a vegetarian.

Uses store cupboard ingredients.

Serves 8   Costs £

2 tbsp cornflour

3 tbsp caster sugar

3 eggs, size 3

1 pt (600 ml) milk

2 tsp vanilla essence

1 Put cornflour, sugar and eggs into a bowl and whisk together until smooth.

2 Bring milk to the boil in a saucepan. Gradually whisk into the cornflour mixture and continue whisking until smooth.

3 Pour milk back into the saucepan and cook over a medium heat, stirring continuously until thickened and smooth.

4 Take off the heat and stir in the vanilla.

To serve now: *serve hot with fruit pies, see p.156 and p.158.*

To freeze: *cool completely. Pour custard into sections of two ice cube trays. Freeze until solid then press cubes into a plastic bag. Seal, label and freeze for 1 month.*

To defrost: *put four cubes per portion into a small saucepan. Defrost for 2 hours at room temperature. Reheat, stirring until hot.*

To microwave: *put four cubes into a small microproof jug, cook on full power for $1\frac{1}{2}$ minutes. Stir once during cooking and just before serving.*

CHILLED DESSERTS

Homemade ice cream

Brown bread ice cream
Coffee ice cream
Chocolate ice cream
Cardamom and peach ice cream

Sorbet

Strawberry sorbet
Blackcurrant sorbet
Apple and mint sorbet
Orange cups
Gooseberry fool
Pineapple meringue crush
Freezeable fruit salad
Chocolate trifle
Lemon and sultana cheesecake
Topsy turvy peach sundae
Apricot ambrosia
Autumn pudding

Homemade ice cream

Basic ice cream recipe

Make up the basic ice cream recipe then add your chosen flavouring from the selection on the following pages.

2 pt (1.1 litre) milk

14 oz (397 g) can full cream condensed milk

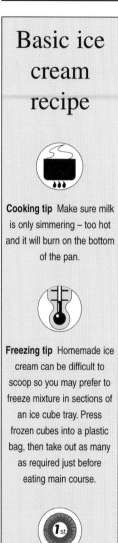

Cooking tip Make sure milk is only simmering – too hot and it will burn on the bottom of the pan.

Freezing tip Homemade ice cream can be difficult to scoop so you may prefer to freeze mixture in sections of an ice cube tray. Press frozen cubes into a plastic bag, then take out as many as required just before eating main course.

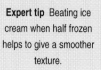

Expert tip Beating ice cream when half frozen helps to give a smoother texture.

I Bring milk to the boil in a saucepan then simmer for 15 minutes. Take off the heat and leave to cool.

2 Strain into a bowl and stir in the condensed milk.

3 Pour into a plastic container and freeze for 4–5 hours until mushy.

4 Beat ice cream well with a fork or transfer to a food processor or liquidiser and blend until smooth.

To freeze: *return ice cream to freezer. Seal, label and freeze until solid. Freeze for 1 month.*

To serve: *take container out of freezer 20 minutes before serving so ice cream can soften. Scoop into dishes and serve.*

Brown bread ice cream

Serves 8   **Costs £**

½ tsp vanilla essence

2 oz (50 g) butter or margarine

4 oz (100 g) fresh brown breadcrumbs

2 oz (50 g) demerara or soft light brown sugar

Suitable for a vegetarian.

1 Make ice cream as basic recipe, add vanilla essence at step 2. Freeze until mushy.

2 Meanwhile heat butter in a frying pan, add breadcrumbs then toss in butter and fry until just beginning to brown. Stir in sugar and fry for a few more minutes until browned and crisp. Cool.

3 Beat ice cream as step 4. Stir in crumb mixture, return to freezer and continue as basic recipe.

Coffee ice cream

Serves 8   **Costs £**

2 tbsp instant coffee

Add coffee to hot milk at end of step 1, stir until dissolved then continue as basic recipe.

Expert tip Use level spoon measures or coffee flavour will be too strong.

Suitable for a vegetarian.

139

Chocolate ice cream

Ingredients tip Use chocolate drops if preferred.

Serves 8   **Costs ££**

6 oz (150 g) packet dark cooking chocolate

Break chocolate into pieces and add to hot milk at end of step 1, stir until melted then continue as basic recipe.

Cardamom and peach ice cream

Ingredients tip Canned apricots can be used instead of peaches in above recipe.

Expert tip Cardamom adds a wonderful flavour, use in apple sauce, fruit compotes and curries too.

Serves 8   **Costs £**

8 cardamom pods

14½ oz (411 g) can peach slices, drained

I   Crush cardamom pods with a rolling pin and add pods and black seeds to milk at beginning of step 1, bring to boil and simmer as basic recipe. Cool, then strain into a bowl.

2   Drain and purée peaches in a liquidiser or food processor. Stir into milk at step 2. Continue as basic recipe.

140

Sorbet

Basic sorbet

Make the most of special offer summer fruit buys from your local market or pick your own farm. Freeze several flavours and serve a small scoop of each one for a refreshingly light dessert.

2 tsp powdered gelatine
6 oz (150 g) granulated sugar
flavourings, see below

1 Put 3 tbsp water into a cup and sprinkle gelatine over. Leave to soak for 5 minutes.

2 Put sugar into a saucepan with ¾ pt (450 ml) water. Slowly bring to the boil, stirring occasionally until sugar has dissolved. Boil rapidly for 3 minutes.

3 Take pan off the heat, add the gelatine and stir until dissolved. Leave to cool.

4 Prepare flavouring, see below, then stir into syrup.

5 Pour into a shallow plastic box, cover and freeze for 4–5 hours until mushy. Beat with a fork or transfer to a food processor or liquidiser and blend until smooth. Return to container.

To freeze: *seal, label and freeze until solid. Freeze for 3–4 months.*

To serve: *remove from freezer 15 minutes before serving so sorbet can soften slightly before scooping.*

Strawberry sorbet

Omit gelatine for vegetarian

Serves 8   Costs £

1½ lb (675 g) strawberries, hulled

1 lemon, finely grated rind and juice

Purée strawberries in a liquidiser or food processor then press purée through a sieve and discard seeds. Stir into sugar syrup at step 4 with lemon rind and juice. Continue as basic recipe.

Expert tip Don't forget to sieve the strawberries or the seeds will spoil the finished sorbet.

Black-currant sorbet

Expert tip If you don't have a food processor or liquidiser then slightly overcook fruit and press small batches through a sieve.

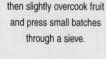

Omit gelatine for vegetarian

Serves 8   Costs £

1½ lb fresh or frozen blackcurrants

1½ oz (40 g) granulated sugar

Remove strings from blackcurrants with a fork and put fruit into a saucepan with sugar and 3 tbsp water. Cover and simmer for 4–5 minutes until soft. Cool then purée in a liquidiser or food processor. Press purée through a sieve and discard the seeds. Stir into sugar syrup at step 4. Continue as basic sorbet recipe.

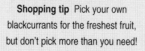

Shopping tip Pick your own blackcurrants for the freshest fruit, but don't pick more than you need!

Healthy tip High in vitamin C.

Apple and mint sorbet

Shopping tip A good way to use up windfall apples.

Ingredients tip Use fresh mint from the garden or ½ tsp dried.

Serves 8   Costs £

1½ lb (450 g) cooking apples
1 oz (25 g) granulated sugar
3 tbsp fresh chopped mint

Quarter, core and peel apples. Roughly chop and put into a saucepan with sugar and 3 tbsp water. Cover and simmer for 10 minutes until apples are soft. Cool then purée in a liquidiser or press through a sieve. Stir into syrup at step 4 with mint. Continue as basic recipe.

Omit gelatine for vegetarian

Orange cups

Freezing tip Take oranges out of freezer 15 minutes before serving, unwrap and put into serving dishes.

Suitable for a vegetarian.

Serves 8   Costs ££

8 small oranges

1 Cut top third off each orange and scoop out fleshy centres to leave eight orange 'cups'. Strain orange juice into a jug and then press flesh through sieve into jug, discarding membrane. Make up to 1 pt (600 ml) with water if needed.

2 Make up sugar syrup with 6 oz (150 g) granulated sugar and ¼ pt (150 ml) water, add gelatine as steps 1 and 2. Continue as basic recipe, adding orange juice at step 4.

3 Spoon beaten sorbet into orange cups at step 5. Put oranges into a dish and open-freeze until solid, about 2 hours. Freeze any remaining sorbet in a small dish.

143

Shopping tip Look out for minneola oranges as they are very juicy with little pith and no pips.

4 Add extra frozen sorbet to orange cups and add lids. Wrap each orange in cling film, put into a plastic box, seal and label. Freeze until required.

Goose-berry fool

Freezing tip If you don't have enough small pots then line ramekin dishes with cling film, fill with fool then seal cling film. Freeze until solid then dip dishes in hot water, loosen with a knife and pack blocks into a plastic box. When ready to serve, take out as many blocks as required. Unwrap and return to ramekin dishes to defrost.

Shopping tip If you buy yogurt in large containers weigh out on kitchen scales or measure $\frac{1}{4}$ pt (150 ml) into a measuring jug.

Serves 8   Costs ££

1½ lb (675 g) gooseberries

4 oz (100 g) granulated sugar

3 tbsp custard powder

¾ pt (450 ml) milk

5 oz (125 g) Greek yogurt

few drops green food colouring

I Top and tail gooseberries with a small pair of scissors. Put gooseberries in a saucepan with 3 oz (75 g) sugar and 3 tbsp water. Cover and simmer for 4–5 minutes until gooseberries are soft. Cool slightly.

2 Purée in a liquidiser or food processor until smooth then press through a sieve and discard the seeds.

3 Mix remaining sugar, custard powder and a little of the milk to a smooth paste. Bring the remaining milk to the boil in rinsed gooseberry pan then stir into custard powder and return milk mixture to the pan.

4 Heat, stirring until thickened and smooth. Pour into gooseberry purée and leave to cool.

5 Stir yogurt and a little colouring into gooseberry mixture.

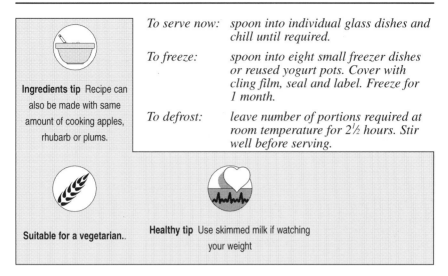

Ingredients tip Recipe can also be made with same amount of cooking apples, rhubarb or plums.

To serve now:	*spoon into individual glass dishes and chill until required.*
To freeze:	*spoon into eight small freezer dishes or reused yogurt pots. Cover with cling film, seal and label. Freeze for 1 month.*
To defrost:	*leave number of portions required at room temperature for 2½ hours. Stir well before serving.*

Suitable for a vegetarian..

Healthy tip Use skimmed milk if watching your weight

Pineapple meringue crush

Quick to make

Expert tip Add defrosting instructions to freezer label.

Suitable for a vegetarian.

Serves 8 Costs £

½ pt (300 ml) whipping cream

14½ oz (432 g) can pineapple pieces

1 pkt of 8 meringue nests

1 Softly whip cream until just beginning to form peaks.

2 Drain pineapple and reserve eight pieces. Finely chop remainder. Fold into cream.

3 Crush meringues into cream mixture using hands. Lightly mix together with a spoon.

4 Line an 8 inch (20 cm) springform tin with 2 long pieces of cling film so base and sides are covered. Pour in meringue mixture, level mixture and arrange reserved pineapple around the edge of the tin to mark portions. Freeze until solid.

5 Remove from freezer, unclip tin, peel off cling film and cut dessert into eight wedges with a hot knife.

Ingredients tip Add
1–2 tbsp chopped glacé
ginger, if liked.

To serve now: *put dessert on to plates, defrost for 10 minutes at room temperature.*

To freeze: *wrap each portion in cling film. Seal, label and pack into a plastic box or bag. Return to freezer and freeze for 3–4 months.*

To defrost: *take out as many portions as required, unwrap, put on serving plates and defrost at room temperature for 20 minutes before serving.*

Freezeable fruit salad

Quick to make.

Shopping tip Shop around for fruit on special offer or market bargains. Compare prices of cartons of orange juice.

Suitable for a vegetarian.

Healthy tip Good supply of vitamin C.

Serves 8   Costs ££

1 medium pineapple

1 small yellow honeydew melon

8 oz (225 g) green grapes

2 ripe peaches, optional

3 oz (75 g) caster sugar

½ pt (300 ml) orange juice

---

1   Cut leafy top off pineapple, slice off base then cut skin off in vertical strips. Cut into eight long wedges then cut away core. Slice and put into a bowl.

2   Halve melon, scoop out seeds then cut into thin wedges and cut away skin. Dice flesh and add to pineapple.

3   Halve grapes and scoop out seeds if needed. Slice peaches, if using and discard stones. Add fruit to bowl with sugar and orange juice. Toss together.

To serve now: *spoon into glass dishes, chill until required.*

To freeze: *divide between eight small plastic boxes or bags. Seal, label and freeze for 4–6 months.*

To defrost: *take out as many portions as required. Defrost for 4 hours at room temperature.*

Chocolate trifle

Quick to make.

Shopping tip Look out for cans of broken mandarin segments, they're much cheaper and great for trifle.

Suitable for a vegetarian.

Ingredients tip Soak sponge in a little sherry if liked.

Serves 8   Costs £

1 small chocolate Swiss roll

11½ oz (312 g) canned broken mandarine segments

1 pt (600 ml) milk

3 tbsp custard powder

2 tbsp caster sugar

3 oz (75 g) dark cooking chocolate

¼ pt (150 ml) whipping cream

I   Cut Swiss roll into eight slices and put a slice in the bottom of eight small foil pudding basins, reused yogurt pots or china ramekin dishes.

2   Drain mandarins and divide between dishes.

3   Pour almost all the milk into a saucepan and bring to the boil. Pour remaining milk into a small bowl and stir in custard powder and caster sugar, mix until a smooth paste. Stir in boiling milk then pour milk back into pan.

4   Cook custard, stirring continuously until thickened and smooth. Take pan off the heat. Grate a little chocolate and reserve for decoration. Break remainder into pieces, add to hot custard and stir until melted.

5   Pour over mandarins and leave to cool.

6   Whip cream until softly peaking then spread over trifles. Sprinkle with reserved grated chocolate.

147

To serve now: chill until required.

To freeze: cover with foil lids, cling film or plastic lids. Seal and label. Freeze for 1 month.

To defrost: uncover and defrost for 3 hours at room temperature.

Lemon and sultana cheese- cake

Shopping tip If you can't get curd cheese then use full fat soft (cream) cheese.

Ingredients tip Can use an orange in place of lemon, raisins in place of sultanas. Soak fruit in a little sherry if liked.

Expert tip Cheesecake may crack as it cools.

Serves 8   Costs ££

Sponge base

2 oz (50 g) soft margarine

2 oz (50 g) caster sugar

2oz (50 g) self-raising flour

1 egg, size 3

Topping

8 oz (225 g) cottage cheese

8 oz (225 g) curd cheese

2 oz (50 g) caster sugar

2 eggs, size 3

¼ pt (150 ml) natural yogurt

1 lemon, grated rind and juice

2 oz (50 g) sultanas

I   Preheat the oven to 350°F, 180°C, Gas 4. Lightly brush an 8 inch (20 cm) springform tin with a little oil and line base with a circle of greaseproof paper.

2   Put all sponge base ingredients together in a bowl and beat together until smooth.

3   Spoon into tin and level surface. Cook for 15 min until pale golden. Set aside while making filling. Reduce oven temperature to 325°F, 160°C, Gas 3.

4 Sieve cottage cheese into a bowl or food processor. Add all remaining ingredients except sultanas and mix together briefly until smooth. Stir in sultanas.

5 Pour mixture into tin, level surface and cook for 45 minutes until lightly browned and just set. Turn off oven and leave cheesecake to cool still in oven.

6 When cold remove from tin and peel off base paper.

To serve now: *transfer to a serving plate and chill well before cutting into wedges.*

To freeze: *cut into eight wedges and wrap each in cling film or foil. Pack into a plastic box, seal, label and freeze for 3–4 months.*

To defrost: *take out as many portions as required, unwrap and put on to a serving plate, recover loosely with wrapping and defrost for 3 hours at room temperature.*

To microwave: *unwrap and put one portion on a microproof plate. Loosely cover with cling film and cook on defrost (30 per cent) for 2 minutes. Leave to stand for 5 minutes.*

Topsy turvy peach sundae

Ingredients tip Can also be made with a can of mandarins or apricots. Or try a strawberry or raspberry jelly with a can of strawberries or raspberries.

Healthy tip This dessert tastes creamy but is virtually fat free.

Expert tip Don't leave moulds in water too long as jelly layer melts faster than fromage frais layer.

Freezing tip Dessert will lose shape if left longer than 2 hours to defrost.

Serves 8   **Costs ££**

4½ oz (135 g) orange jelly
10½ oz (411 g) can peach slices
1 lb 2 oz (500 g) tub fatless fromage frais
2 oz (50 g) caster sugar
4 oz (100 g) digestive biscuits
2 oz (50 g) soft margarine

---

1 Cut jelly into pieces and put into a saucepan with 6 tbsp water. Heat gently until melted.

2 Meanwhile drain peaches, put eight slices on a board and cut each into 3 thin slices. Arrange three slices in the base of eight individual ramekin dishes.

3 Add 2 tsp melted jelly to each dish. Chill for 20 minutes until set.

4 Purée remaining peaches in a food processor or liquidiser. Mix with fromage frais and sugar.

5 When jelly in moulds has set, gently warm remaining jelly until melted and stir into fromage frais mixture. Spoon into moulds.

6 Crush biscuits in a plastic bag. Melt margarine in washed jelly pan then stir in crumbs and mix well. Spoon over moulds and press lightly into fromage frais mixture. Chill until set.

To serve now: dip moulds in boiling water, count to 10 then turn out on to small plates.

To freeze: open-freeze until solid. Dip moulds in water as above, and count to 30. Turn out and wrap in cling film. Seal, label and pack into a plastic box. Freeze for 3–4 months.

To defrost: *remove wrappings and place dessert, jelly uppermost on a small serving plate. Defrost at room temperature for 2 hours.*

Apricot ambrosia

Serves 8   Costs £

2 pt (1.1 litre) milk

4 oz (100 g) pudding rice

2 oz (50 g) caster sugar

2 tsp vanilla essence

13½ oz (411 g) can apricots halves

Cooking tip Watch the temperature or milk may catch on base of pan.

Expert tip Stir cooling rice mixture occasionally so that a skin doesn't form.

Ingredients tip Use 1lb (450 g) fresh fruit, poached with a little water then puréed, if preferred.

1 Put milk and rice into a saucepan and bring to the boil, stirring. Cover and simmer for 40 minutes, stirring occasionally until rice is soft and creamy.

2 Take pan off the heat and stir in the sugar and vanilla. Leave to cool, stirring occasionally.

3 Meanwhile, drain and purée apricots in a liquidiser or food processor.

4 Spoon a layer of rice in the base of eight recycled yogurt pots (or glass dishes if serving now). Divide half the apricot purée between dishes then top with remaining rice and remaining apricot purée.

To serve now: *chill until required.*

To freeze: *wrap with cling film, seal well and label. Freeze for 1 month.*

To defrost: *leave at room temperature for 4 hours.*

To microwave: *pierce cling film and cook one at a time on defrost (30 per cent) for 3 minutes. Stand for 10 minutes.*

Autumn pudding

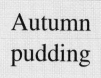

Serves 8   **Costs £**

2½ lb (1.1 kg) cooking apples

9 oz (250 g) blackberries

6 oz (150 g) caster sugar

20 medium cut slices white bread

Ingredients tip A good recipe to use up windfall apples and hedgerow blackberries. Use fresh or frozen blackcurrants if blackberries are unavailable.

Expert tip Make sure metal weights cannot touch bread or fruit acids will react with metal. If you don't have enough cooking weights then use cans from the cupboard.

Suitable for a vegetarian.

I   Quarter, core, peel and thinly slice apples. Put into a saucepan with the blackberries, sugar and ¾ pt (450 ml) water.

2   Cover and simmer for 15 minutes until apples are just soft.

3   Drain off the juice into a shallow dish.

4   Line eight cups, ramekins or metal moulds with cling film. Stamp out eight small bread rounds with a small biscuit cutter from two slices bread.

5   Dip rounds in fruit juice then place, juice side downwards in base of dishes.

6   Reserve eight slices bread and cut crusts off remaining bread. Cut each slice of trimmed bread in half then each half into four strips.

7   Dip each strip into juice then press on to sides of dishes, so juice side is touching cling film. Overlap strips slightly and butt closely up to bread in bottom of dish.

8   Continue until all dishes are lined. Spoon in fruit and moisten with the juice.

9   Cut circles of bread the same size as top of dishes. Dip in any remaining juice and place on top of dishes. Fold cling film over the top of dishes.

10   Add a square of cling film to top of each dish then weight down and chill overnight.

To serve now: *remove weights and top piece of cling film. Unfold cling film, invert dish on to a plate and remove dish. Peel off cling film and serve with spoonfuls of natural yogurt.*

To freeze: *lift puddings out of dishes. Seal cling film, label and freeze for 3–4 months.*

To defrost: *take out as many as required and put on to individual serving plates. Defrost for 3 hours at room temperature. Remove cling film just before serving.*

To microwave: *put one pudding on to a microproof serving plate, peel off cling film and lay over pudding. Cook on defrost (30 per cent) for 5 minutes. Stand 5 minutes before serving.*

HOT PUDDINGS

Toffeed prune and apricot compôte

Quick to make.

Shopping tip Long life cartons of orange juice vary in price, bulk buy bargains.

Expert tip Don't stir sugar when making toffee or it will crystallise

Suitable for a vegetarian.

Serves 8   Costs ££

9 oz (250 g) pkt ready to eat stoned prunes

5 oz (125 g) ready to eat dried apricots

¼ pt (150 ml) long life orange juice

3 oz soft light brown sugar

1 tbsp golden syrup

2 tsp cornflour

2 oz (50 g) soft margarine

I Halve prunes and cut apricots into strips. Put into a saucepan with the orange juice and ¼ pt (150 ml) water. Bring to the boil and simmer for 10 minutes. Set aside.

2 Put sugar and syrup into a saucepan and heat very gently, without stirring until sugar has dissolved. Increase the heat and cook for 3–4 minutes until mixture has just changed colour.

3 Meanwhile mix the cornflour with a little water until a smooth paste then make up to ½ pt (300 ml) with more water.

4 As soon as sugar has changed colour, quickly take pan off the heat, add the margarine then pour in the cornflour mixture and stand well back. When bubbles have subsided a little, stir well.

5 Pour toffee sauce over fruit.

To serve now: *spoon into bowls and serve warm or cold.*

To freeze: *cool completely then pack portions into small plastic bags. Seal, label and freeze for 4–6 months.*

To defrost: *take out as many portions as required, defrost for 3 hours at room temperature.*

155

Serving tip Serve with fromage frais, it has a much longer fridge life than cream and is cheaper and healthier too.

Remove bags, transfer to a saucepan and reheat.

To microwave: peel bag off portion, put into a micro-proof serving dish, cover loosely with bag and cook on full power for 1½ minutes.

Mince-meat and apple dumplings

Ingredients tip Use small windfall apples or pick out the smallest cooking apples in the supermarket.

Varying ingredients tip For those with small appetites, cut pastry into 12, roll out thinly. Divide mincemeat between centres of squares, top with six halved apples and continue as recipe.

Serves 8   Costs ££

1¼ lb (550 g) plain flour

5 oz (125 g) block margarine

5 oz (125 g) white vegetable fat

8 small cooking apples, about 2¾ lb (1.2 kg)

8 oz (225 g) mincemeat

4 oz (100 g) caster sugar

1 size 3 egg, beaten

1 Preheat the oven to 375°F, 190°C, Gas 5. Lightly grease a large baking sheet.

2 Put flour and a little salt into a bowl, add fats cut into pieces and rub in with finger-tips or an electric mixer until fine crumbs.

3 Mix to a smooth dough with 6 tbsp water. Knead lightly and cut into eight pieces.

4 Peel and core apples.

5 Roll out one piece of pastry thinly on a lightly floured surface and trim to a 7 inch (18 cm) square, or square large enough to enclose apple.

6 Put apple in the centre, spoon one eigth of the mincemeat into the apple centre and sprinkle apple with 2 tsp sugar.

Freezing tip Pack into a large plastic box so dumplings don't get crushed or add coloured labels marked fragile.

Vegetarian tip Choose a brand of mincemeat made with vegetable suet, check label before use.

Expert tip Best not to reheat in the microwave as pastry can toughen.

7 Brush pastry edges with egg then draw corners of pastry up and over apple and pinch all edges together. Put on to baking sheet and repeat with remaining apples.

8 Reroll any pastry trimmings, cut leaves and add to dumplings. Brush pastry with egg and sprinkle with remaining sugar.

9 Cook for 25 minutes until golden brown.

To serve now: serve hot with custard.

To freeze: cool completely then wrap in foil. Seal, label and freeze for 3–4 months.

To defrost: cook from frozen, still in foil at 400°F, 200°C, Gas 6 for 20 minutes. Open out foil, cook for 10 minutes.

Swiss apple tart

Suitable for a vegetarian.

Ingredients tip Sprinkle top with a few flaked almonds before cooking if liked.

Serves 8   Costs £

Pastry

8 oz (225 g) plain flour

2 oz (50 g) block margarine

2 oz (50 g) white vegetable fat

Filling

1¼ lb (550 g) cooking apples

3 eggs, size 3, beaten

3 oz (75 g) caster sugar

1 lemon, grated rind and juice

I Preheat the oven to 375°F, 190°C, Gas 5. Put flour and a little salt into a bowl. Add

157

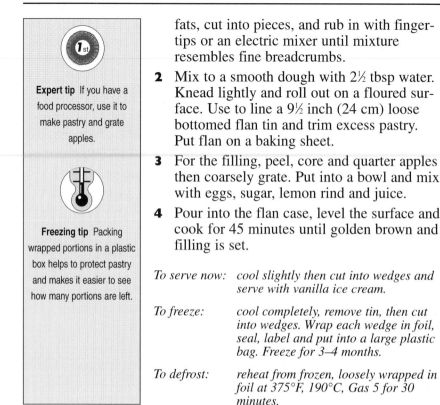

fats, cut into pieces, and rub in with finger-tips or an electric mixer until mixture resembles fine breadcrumbs.

2 Mix to a smooth dough with 2½ tbsp water. Knead lightly and roll out on a floured sur-face. Use to line a 9½ inch (24 cm) loose bottomed flan tin and trim excess pastry. Put flan on a baking sheet.

3 For the filling, peel, core and quarter apples then coarsely grate. Put into a bowl and mix with eggs, sugar, lemon rind and juice.

4 Pour into the flan case, level the surface and cook for 45 minutes until golden brown and filling is set.

To serve now: *cool slightly then cut into wedges and serve with vanilla ice cream.*

To freeze: *cool completely, remove tin, then cut into wedges. Wrap each wedge in foil, seal, label and put into a large plastic bag. Freeze for 3–4 months.*

To defrost: *reheat from frozen, loosely wrapped in foil at 375°F, 190°C, Gas 5 for 30 minutes.*

Double crust rhubarb and ginger pies

Serves 8   Costs ££

2 lb (900 g) rhubarb

4 oz (100 g) caster sugar

Pastry

1½ lb (675 g) plain flour

1½ tsp ground ginger

6 oz (150 g) block margarine

6 oz (150 g) white vegetable fat

To glaze

2 tbsp milk

extra caster sugar

Cooking tip If using a fan assisted oven you may need to cover pies with foil after 15 minutes to prevent pastry overbrowning.

Expert tip You may need to cook pies on two baking sheets depending on the size of your oven. Swop them over half way through cooking for even browning.

1 Preheat the oven to 375°F, 190°C, Gas 5. Trim, wash and thinly slice rhubarb. Put into a bowl and mix with the sugar.

2 To make the pastry, put the flour into a bowl with a little salt and the ginger. Cut the fats into pieces, add to flour and rub in with fingertips or an electric mixer until the mixture resembles fine breadcrumbs.

3 Mix to a smooth dough with 7–8 tbsp water. Knead lightly. Cut pastry into eight, then cut one third off each piece.

4 Roll out one of the larger pieces of dough thinly on a floured surface and use to line an individual foil pie dish. Trim off excess pastry and add to a smaller piece of dough.

5 Repeat until eight pie dishes are lined. Divide rhubarb between dishes and brush pastry edges with a little water.

6 Roll out each small piece of dough in turn and use to cover pies, pressing edges together well. Trim away excess pastry. Reroll trimmings and cut leaves or pretty shapes with tiny biscuit cutters and arrange on pies.

7 Brush pastry with milk and sprinkle with sugar. Put pies on a large baking sheet and cook for 20–25 minutes until golden.

To serve now: *serve hot with custard.*

To freeze: *cool completely then overwrap with cling film. Seal, label and freeze for 3–4 months.*

To defrost: *defrost as many as required for 3 hours at room temperature then reheat at 350°F, 180°C, Gas 4 for 30 minutes.*

159

Apple and blackberry cobbler

Ingredients tip Pick your blackberries from the hedgerow or if out of season use frozen mixed summer fruits.

Cooking tip Make in two batches if you have only one tin.

Expert tip Brush with a little milk and sugar if preferred.

Suitable for a vegetarian.

Serves 8 Costs £

Pastry

1 lb (450 g) plain flour

4 oz (100 g) block margarine

4 oz (100 g) white vegetable fat

Filling

2 lb (900 g) cooking apples

4 oz (100 g) caster sugar

4 tsp cornflour

6 oz (150 g) blackberries

1 egg, size 3, beaten

extra sugar to sprinkle

I Preheat the oven to 375°F, 190°C, Gas 5. Put flour and a pinch of salt into a bowl. Add fats, cut into pieces, and rub in with fingertips or an electric mixer until the mixtue resembles fine breadcrumbs.

2 Mix to a smooth dough with 4–5 tbsp water. Knead lightly then cut pastry into eight.

3 Quarter, core and peel apples. Thinly slice and put into a bowl with sugar and cornflour, toss together.

4 Roll out one piece of pastry on a lightly floured surface until a rough circle about the size of a 6 inch (15 cm) saucer.

5 Lay circle in one section of a large four section Yorkshire pudding tin. Add one quarter of the apple mixture and one quarter of the blackberries. Fold pastry up and around fruit leaving centre of pie open.

6 Repeat to make eight pies in two, four section tins. Brush pastry with beaten egg and sprinkle with sugar.

Freezing tip Add a coloured label marked fragile to protect pies.

Cook for 20 minutes until pastry is golden and fruit is cooked.

To serve now: *carefully take pies out of tins and serve with custard.*

To freeze: *cool completely then open-freeze in tins. Loosen with a knife then remove. Wrap individually in foil, seal, label and freeze for 3–4 months.*

To defrost: *unwrap as many frozen portions as required and put on a baking sheet, recover tops with foil and cook from frozen at 375°F, 190°C, Gas 5 for 40 minutes. Or defrost for 4 hours at room temperature then cook for 15 minutes.*

Adam's pudding

Expert tip A version of the favourite Eve's pudding made with apple and lemon.

Freezing tip Don't use foil containers as fruit acids may pit the surface. Recycle cook-chill plastic dishes, cutting double ones into two if needed.

Serves 8   Costs £

1½ lb (675 g) plums

7 oz (200 g) caster sugar

4 oz (100 g) soft margarine

4 oz (100 g) self-raising flour

2 eggs, size 3

1 orange, grated rind and juice

icing sugar to dust

I Preheat the oven to 350°F, 180°C, Gas 4. Wash plums, slice and discard stones. Put into a saucepan with 3 oz (75 g) caster sugar and 4 tbsp water. Cook uncovered for 10 minutes until plums are just cooked.

2 Put remaining sugar into a bowl with margarine, flour and eggs and beat together until smooth.

3 Stir orange rind into plums and 3 tbsp juice into egg mixture.

4 Spoon plums into eight individual ovenproof

161

dishes with a little of the juice. Top with sponge mixture and level the surface of each.

5 Put dishes on a baking tray and cook for 15 minutes until risen and golden brown. Dust with sifted icing sugar.

To serve now: serve hot with custard.

To freeze: cool completely then overwrap dishes with foil or cling film. Seal, label and freeze for 3–4 months.

To defrost: remove wrapping, loosely cover with foil, cook from frozen at 375°F, 190°C, Gas 5 for 30 minutes.

To microwave: cook one at a time in a microproof dish covered with pierced cling film on full power for 3 minutes.

Plum and marzipan crumble

Shopping tip Alternate fruits depending on what is a good buy, apples, rhubarb and gooseberries are also delicious.

Serves 8   Costs ££

2 lb (900 g) plums

4 oz (100 g) caster sugar

Topping

8 oz (225 g) plain flour

2 oz (50 g) caster sugar

4 oz (100 g) block margarine

4 oz (100 g) marzipan

I Wash plums, slice and discard stones. Put into a saucepan with the sugar and 3 tbsp water. Cook uncovered for 10 minutes until plums are just cooked.

2 To make topping, put flour into a bowl with the sugar. Add margarine cut into pieces and rub in with fingertips or an electric mixer until the mixtue resembles fine breadcrumbs.

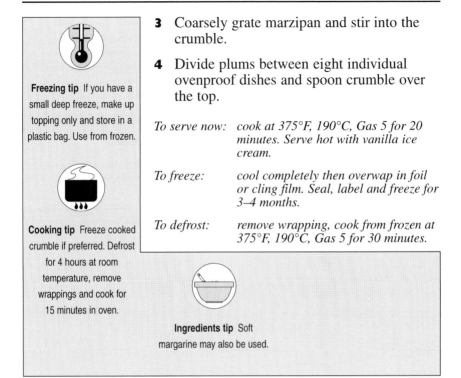

Freezing tip If you have a small deep freeze, make up topping only and store in a plastic bag. Use from frozen.

Cooking tip Freeze cooked crumble if preferred. Defrost for 4 hours at room temperature, remove wrappings and cook for 15 minutes in oven.

Ingredients tip Soft margarine may also be used.

3 Coarsely grate marzipan and stir into the crumble.

4 Divide plums between eight individual ovenproof dishes and spoon crumble over the top.

To serve now: *cook at 375°F, 190°C, Gas 5 for 20 minutes. Serve hot with vanilla ice cream.*

To freeze: *cool completely then overwap in foil or cling film. Seal, label and freeze for 3–4 months.*

To defrost: *remove wrapping, cook from frozen at 375°F, 190°C, Gas 5 for 30 minutes.*

VARIATIONS

Choc chip crumble

Make up topping as above but omit marzipan and add 3 oz (75 g) dark or milk chocolate dots. Spoon over cooked plums or apples.

Orange and coconut crumble

Make up topping as above but omit marzipan and stir in the grated rind of 1 orange and 3 oz (75 g) desiccated coconut. Spoon over cooked rhubarb, apples, gooseberries or plums. Check halfway through baking and cover with foil, if needed, as coconut tends to brown quickly.

Oaty ginger crumble

Make up crumble with 8 oz (225 g) malted brown flour, 2 oz (50 g) demerara or soft brown sugar and 4 oz (100 g) margarine as above. Omit marzipan and stir in 2 oz (50 g) oats and 1 tsp ground ginger. Spoon over cooked apple or rhubarb.

Sticky date and toffee pudding

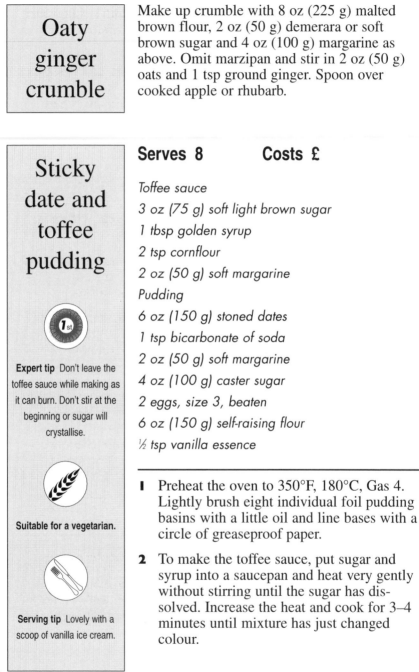

Expert tip Don't leave the toffee sauce while making as it can burn. Don't stir at the beginning or sugar will crystallise.

Suitable for a vegetarian.

Serving tip Lovely with a scoop of vanilla ice cream.

Serves 8   Costs £

Toffee sauce

3 oz (75 g) soft light brown sugar

1 tbsp golden syrup

2 tsp cornflour

2 oz (50 g) soft margarine

Pudding

6 oz (150 g) stoned dates

1 tsp bicarbonate of soda

2 oz (50 g) soft margarine

4 oz (100 g) caster sugar

2 eggs, size 3, beaten

6 oz (150 g) self-raising flour

½ tsp vanilla essence

I Preheat the oven to 350°F, 180°C, Gas 4. Lightly brush eight individual foil pudding basins with a little oil and line bases with a circle of greaseproof paper.

2 To make the toffee sauce, put sugar and syrup into a saucepan and heat very gently without stirring until the sugar has dissolved. Increase the heat and cook for 3–4 minutes until mixture has just changed colour.

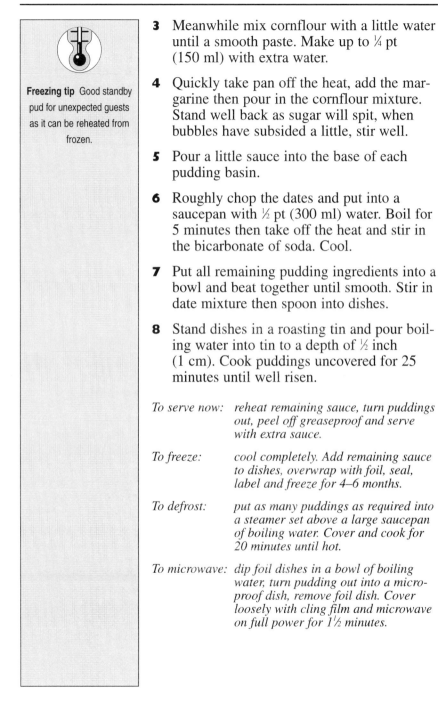

3 Meanwhile mix cornflour with a little water until a smooth paste. Make up to ¼ pt (150 ml) with extra water.

4 Quickly take pan off the heat, add the margarine then pour in the cornflour mixture. Stand well back as sugar will spit, when bubbles have subsided a little, stir well.

5 Pour a little sauce into the base of each pudding basin.

6 Roughly chop the dates and put into a saucepan with ½ pt (300 ml) water. Boil for 5 minutes then take off the heat and stir in the bicarbonate of soda. Cool.

7 Put all remaining pudding ingredients into a bowl and beat together until smooth. Stir in date mixture then spoon into dishes.

8 Stand dishes in a roasting tin and pour boiling water into tin to a depth of ½ inch (1 cm). Cook puddings uncovered for 25 minutes until well risen.

To serve now: *reheat remaining sauce, turn puddings out, peel off greaseproof and serve with extra sauce.*

To freeze: *cool completely. Add remaining sauce to dishes, overwrap with foil, seal, label and freeze for 4–6 months.*

To defrost: *put as many puddings as required into a steamer set above a large saucepan of boiling water. Cover and cook for 20 minutes until hot.*

To microwave: *dip foil dishes in a bowl of boiling water, turn pudding out into a microproof dish, remove foil dish. Cover loosely with cling film and microwave on full power for 1½ minutes.*

Bread pudding

Suitable for a vegetarian.

Ingredients tip If you don't have enough cinnamon then use cinnamon and nutmeg or all mixed spice.

Cooking tip If you have a fan assisted oven you may need to cover pudding with foil after 30 minutes to prevent overbrowning.

Expert tip Leave surface of pudding craggy so it cooks to a wonderful sugary crisp crust.

Freezing tip Don't defrost in the microwave as pudding goes 'gluey'.

Serves 8 Costs £

1 sliced white loaf

¾ pt (450 ml) milk

5 oz (125 g) soft margarine

5 oz (125 g) soft light brown sugar

3 tsp ground cinnamon

8 oz (225 g) mixed dried fruit

1 Break bread into pieces and put into a large bowl. Pour over milk and ¾ pt (450 ml) water and leave to soak for 45 minutes.

2 Preheat the oven to 350°F, 180°C, Gas 4. Grease a 7 × 11 × 1½ inch (18 × 28 × 4 cm) small roasting tin with a little of the margarine.

3 Add 4 oz (100 g) margarine, 3 oz (75 g) sugar and cinnamon to bread and beat with a wooden spoon or squeeze together with hands until well mixed. Stir in fruit.

4 Spoon mixture into tin, dot with the remaining margarine and sprinkle over remaining sugar. Cook for 1¼ hours until golden brown.

To serve now: cut into thick slices and serve hot with Tangy lemon sauce, see p.134 or a little single cream.

To freeze: cool completely. Cut into thick slices and wrap each in foil. Seal, label and pack into a large plastic bag. Freeze for 3–4 months.

To defrost: reheat from frozen, loosely wrapped in foil at 400°F, 200°C, Gas 6 for 30 minutes.

Brown betty

Ingredients tip Flavour crumbs with ground cinnamon if liked.

Cooking tip Don't leave crumbs unattended while frying or they may burn.

Suitable for a vegetarian.

Serves 8   Costs £

3 oz (75 g) soft margarine

2 tbsp oil

8 oz (225 g) fresh breadcrumbs

2 oz (50 g) oats

8 oz (225 g) soft brown sugar

2 lb (900 g) cooking apples

I Heat butter and oil in a large saucepan, add breadcrumbs, oats and 6 oz (150 g) sugar and fry stirring until golden. Set aside.

2 Quarter, core and peel apples. Thinly slice and put into a separate saucepan with 6 tbsp water. Cover and cook for 5 minutes until soft.

3 Spoon half the crumb mixture into the base of eight ovenproof dishes. Add apple then cover with remaining breadcrumbs.

To serve now: cook at 375°F, 190°C, Gas 5 for 15 minutes. Serve hot with vanilla ice cream or custard.

To freeze: cool completely then wrap in foil or cling film. Seal, label and freeze for for 3–4 months.

To defrost: cook from frozen, loosely covered with foil at 375°F, 190°C, Gas 5 for 30 minutes.

To microwave: cover microproof dish with pierced cling, cook one portion at a time on full power for 2½ minutes.

167

TEATIME TRAYBAKES

Oaty apple and banana bars
Sticky marmalade gingerbread
Fruity slices
Spiced carrot cake
Mocha squares

Oaty apple and banana bars

Cuts into 18   Costs £

1 × 8 oz (225 g) cooking apple

6 oz (150 g) soft margarine

6 oz (150 g) soft light brown sugar

8 oz (225 g) porridge oats

2 oz (50 g) banana chips

Expert tip Don't grease tin with soft margarine or flapjack will stick. Better to use cooking oil.

Ingredients tip Buy banana chips from health food shops. Omit if unavailable.

Suitable for a vegetarian.

I   Preheat oven to 400°F, 200°C, Gas 6. Grease and base line a small 7 × 11 × 1½ inch (18 × 28 × 4 cm) roasting tin with greaseproof paper.

2   Quarter, core, peel and finely chop apple. Melt margarine in a saucepan, add apple and fry gently for 2–3 minutes until softened.

3   Add sugar and oats. Break banana chips into small pieces add to pan and stir mixture well.

4   Spoon into tin and press flat. Cook for 20 minutes until golden brown. Take from oven, mark into bars and leave to cool completely.

5   Take out of tin, peel off paper and cut into bars.

To serve now: *arrange bars on a serving plate. Store any remaining bars in a plastic box for 3–4 days.*

To freeze: *pack bars into a plastic box, interleaving layers with greaseproof paper. Seal, label and freeze for 4–6 months.*

To defrost: *take out as many bars as required. Defrost at room temperature for 2 hours.*

To microwave: *cook one piece at a time on full power for 20 seconds. Cool slightly before serving.*

Sticky marmalade gingerbread

Ingredients tip Use half white and half brown flour if liked.

Cooking tip Can also be made in an 8 inch (20 cm) square cake tin. Cook for about 1 hour.

Expert tip Make into a quick pudding by serving hot with a speedy marmalade sauce made by reheating a few spoonfuls of marmalade with a little orange juice and topped with a scoop of ice cream.

Suitable for a vegetarian.

Cuts into 18   Costs £

4 oz (100 g) soft margarine

3 oz (75 g) granulated sugar

8 oz (225 g) golden syrup

2 tbsp marmalade

8 oz (225 g) self-raising flour

2 tsp ground ginger

½ tsp bicarbonate of soda

¼ pt (150 ml) milk

2 eggs, size 3

---

1 Preheat oven to 350°F, 180°C, Gas 4. Grease and base line a small 7 × 11 × 1½ inch (18 × 28 × 4 cm) roasting tin with greaseproof paper.

2 Put margarine, sugar, syrup and marmalade into a saucepan and heat, stirring until margarine has melted and sugar dissolved. Take off heat and cool slightly.

3 Mix flour, ginger and bicarbonate of soda together then stir into cooled margarine mixture.

4 Beat milk and eggs together then stir into ginger mixture. Pour into tin, level surface and cook for 25 minutes until well risen and golden. Top of cake will spring back when pressed with fingertips if ready.

5 Leave to cool in tin. When cold, take out of tin, peel off paper and cut into bars.

To serve now: *arrange on a serving plate. Store any remaining gingerbread in a plastic box for 6–7 days.*

To freeze: *pack gingerbread into a plastic box, interleaving layers with greaseproof paper. Seal, label and freeze for 4–6 months.*

To defrost: *take out as many pieces of ginger-bread as required. Defrost for 2 hours at room temperature.*

To microwave: cook one piece at a time, on full power for 30 seconds. Cool slightly before serving.

Fruity slices

Cooking tip If you have a fan oven you may need to cover cake with foil halfway through cooking to prevent overbrowning.

Expert tip Drizzle random lines of glacé icing made with a little orange juice over top of cake if liked. open-freeze until solid then pack into a plastic box.

Suitable for a vegetarian.

Cuts into 18   Costs £

5 oz (125 g) soft margarine

5 oz (125 g) caster sugar

6 oz (150 g) self-raising flour

2 eggs, size 3

grated rind of 1 orange

2 tbsp milk

6 oz (150 g) mixed dried fruit

2 tbsp demerara sugar

I Preheat oven to 325°F, 170°C, Gas 3. Grease and base line a small 7 × 11 × 1½ inch (18 × 28 × 4 cm) roasting tin with greaseproof paper.

2 Put margarine, caster sugar, flour, eggs, orange rind and milk into a bowl and beat with a wooden spoon or electric mixer until smooth. Stir in fruit.

3 Spoon into tin, level surface and sprinkle with demerara sugar. Cook for 30 minutes until well risen and golden. Top of cake will spring back when pressed with fingertips if ready.

4 Leave to cool in tin. When cold take out of tin, peel off paper and cut into bars.

To serve now: arrange on a serving plate. Store any remaining slices in a plastic box for 2 days.

To freeze: pack slices into a plastic box, interleaving layers with greaseproof paper. Seal, label and freeze for 4–6 months.

To defrost: take out as many slices as required. Defrost at room temperature for 2 hours.

To microwave: cook one piece at a time on full power for 30 seconds. Cool slightly before serving.

Spiced carrot cake

Expert tip If you have a food processor then use it to grate carrots, mix cake and topping.

Serving tip Serve uniced if preferred. Traditionally topped with cream cheese but orange topping above is much cheaper and just as nice.

Cuts into 24　　Costs £

9 oz (250 g) carrots

6 oz (150 g) soft margarine

6 oz (150 g) soft light brown sugar

6 oz (150 g) self-raising flour

½ tsp baking powder

½ tsp ground ginger

1 tsp ground cinnamon

1 tbsp lemon juice

3 eggs, size 3

Topping

3 oz (75 g) soft margarine

6 oz (150 g) icing sugar

1 tbsp orange or lemon juice

ground cinnamon for sprinkling

---

1 Preheat the oven to 325°F, 170°C, Gas 3. Grease and base line a small 7 × 11 × 1½ inch (18 × 28 × 4 cm) roasting tin with greaseproof paper.

2 Peel and finely grate carrots.

3 Put all remaining cake ingredients into a bowl and beat together with a wooden spoon or electric mixer until smooth.

4 Stir in carrots. Spoon mixture into tin and level surface. Cook for 30 minutes until well risen and golden. Top of cake will spring back when pressed with fingertips if cake is ready.

5 Leave to cool in tin. When cold take out of tin, peel off paper and turn over so top is uppermost.

6 Put topping ingredients into a bowl and beat together until light and fluffy. Spread over top of cake, sprinkle with cinnamon then cut into squares.

To serve now: *arrange on a serving plate. Store any remaining squares in a plastic box for 2 days.*

To freeze: *open-freeze on a tray until topping is hard. Pack into a plastic box, interleaving layers with greaseproof paper. Seal, label and freeze for 3–4 months.*

To defrost: *take out as many squares as required. Defrost in a single layer for 2 hours at room temperature.*

Mocha squares

Expert tip If icing seems to stiff too spread, put pan back on heat and stir until softened.

Ingredients tip Top with melted cake covering instead of fudge icing if prefered.

Cuts into 24   Costs £

1 oz (25 g) cocoa

3 tbsp boiling water

5 oz (125 g) soft margarine

5 oz (125 g) caster sugar

5 oz (125 g) self-raising flour

2 size 3 eggs

2 tbsp milk

1 tsp baking powder

Topping:

2 tsp instant coffee

1 tbsp boiling water

2 oz (50 g) soft margarine

4 oz (100 g) soft light brown sugar

3 tbsp milk

4 oz (100 g) icing sugar, sifted

I Preheat the oven to 325°F, 170°C, Gas 3. Grease and base line a small 7 × 11 × 1½ inch (18 × 28 × 4 cm) roasting tin with greaseproof paper.

2 Put cocoa into a small bowl, add boiling water and mix to a smooth thick paste.

3 Put remaining cake ingredients into a bowl and beat with a wooden spoon or electric mixer until smooth. Stir in cocoa mixture.

4 Spoon into tin and level surface. Cook for 25 minutes until well risen and browned. Top of cake will spring back when pressed with the fingertips if ready.

5 Leave to cool in tin. When cold, take out of tin, peel off paper then turn cake over so top is uppermost.

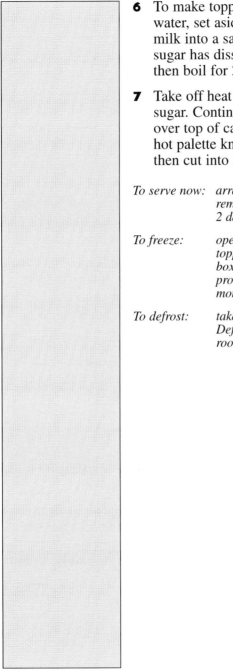

6 To make topping, dissolve coffee in boiling water, set aside. Put margarine, sugar and milk into a saucepan. Heat gently until sugar has dissolved and margarine melted, then boil for 2 minutes.

7 Take off heat and beat in coffee and icing sugar. Continue beating until smooth. Pour over top of cake and quickly spread with a hot palette knife. Leave to cool and harden then cut into squares.

To serve now: *arrange on a serving plate. Store any remaining squares in a plastic box for 2 days.*

To freeze: *open-freeze squares on a tray until topping is hard. Pack into a plastic box, interleaving layers with grease-proof. Seal, label and freeze for 3–4 months.*

To defrost: *take out as many squares as required. Defrost in a single layer for 2 hours at room temperature.*

About Age Concern

Freezing Food on a Budget is one of a wide range of publications produced by Age Concern England, the National Council on Ageing. Age Concern England is actively engaged in training, information provision, fundraising and campaigning for retired people and those who work with them, and also in the provision of products and services such as insurance for older people.

A network of over 1,400 local Age Concern groups, with the support of around 250,000 volunteers, aims to improve the quality of life for older people and develop services appropriate to local needs and resources. These include advice and information, day care, visiting services, transport schemes, clubs, and specialist facilities for older people who are physically and mentally frail.

Age Concern England is a registered charity dependent on public support for the continuation and development of its work.

Age Concern England
1268 London Road
London SW16 4ER
Tel: 0181-679 8000

Age Concern Cymru
4th Floor
1 Cathedral Road
Cardiff CF1 9SD
Tel: 01222 371566

Age Concern Scotland
113 Rose Street
Edinburgh EH2 3DT
Tel: 0131-220 3345

Age Concern Northern Ireland
3 Lower Crescent
Belfast BT7 1NR
Tel: 01232 245729

Publications from ACE Books

A wide range of titles is published by Age Concern England under the ACE Books imprint

Money Matters

Your Taxes and Savings: A guide for older people.
Peta Hodge and Sally West
    This definitive annual guide to financial planning provides a comprehensive explanation of the impact of taxation on the finances of older people. It also looks at managing retirement income and evaluates the wide range of investment opportunities available. Advice is given on building an investment portfolio and seven model portfolios are included.
    Further information on application

Your Rights: A guide to money benefits for older people

Sally West
    A highly acclaimed annual guide to the State benefits available to older people. Contains current information on Income Support, Incapacity Benefit, Housing Benefit, Council Tax Benefit, and paying for residential care, among other matters, and provides advice on how to claim them.
    Further information on application.

Housing

A Buyer's Guide to Retirement Housing
    Buying a flat or bungalow in a sheltered scheme? The new edition of this successful guide provides vital information on the running costs, location, design and management of schemes to help you make an informed decision.
    Co-published with the National Housing and Town Planning Council £4.95 0-86242-127-6

Housing Options for Older People

David Bookbinder

A review of housing options is part of growing older. All the possibilities and their practical implications are carefully considered in this comprehensive guide. £4.95 0-86242-108-X

If you would like to order any of these titles, please write to the Mail Order Unit, Age Concern England, London SW16 4EX, enclosing a cheque or money order for the appropriate amount made payable to Age Concern England. Credit card orders may be made on 0181-679 8000.

Information factsheets

Age Concern England produces over 30 factsheets on a variety of subjects.

To order factsheets

Single copies are available free on receipt of a C5 sae. If you require a selection of factsheets or multiple copies totalling more than five, charges will be given on request.

A complete set of factsheets is available in a ring binder at a cost of £36, which includes the first year's subscription. The current cost for annual subscription for subsequent years is £17. There are different rates of subscription for people living outside the UK. For further information, or to order factsheets, write to:

Information and Policy Department
Age Concern England
1268 London Road
London SW16 4ER